Artful
Appliqué II

Artful
Appliqué II

Introducing Scrapliqué and 12 New Floral Designs

Jane Townswick

Martingale®
& COMPANY

Artful Appliqué II: Introducing Scrapliqué
and 12 New Floral Designs
© 2009 by Jane Townswick

That Patchwork Place® is an imprint of Martingale & Company®.

Martingale & Company
20205 144th Ave. NE
Woodinville, WA 98072-8478 USA
www.martingale-pub.com

Printed in China
14 13 12 11 10 09   8 7 6 5 4 3 2 1

**Library of Congress Cataloging-in-Publication Data
is available upon request.**

ISBN: 978-1-56477-921-2

CREDITS

President & CEO: Tom Wierzbicki
Editor in Chief: Mary V. Green
Managing Editor: Tina Cook
Developmental Editor: Karen Costello Soltys
Technical Editor: Laurie Baker
Copy Editor: Marcy Heffernan
Design Director: Stan Green
Production Manager: Regina Girard
Illustrator: Laurel Strand
Cover & Text Designer: Stan Green
Photographer: Brent Kane

MISSION STATEMENT

Dedicated to providing quality products and service
to inspire creativity.

DEDICATION

To my brother, Gary Townswick, who is a true master artist. I thank you for your kindness and generosity in teaching me about color, composition, and artistic techniques, and for showing me how artistic concepts like color repetition can be used in hand appliqué.

ACKNOWLEDGMENTS

My heartfelt thanks to Dot Murdoch and Teri Weed for lending their valuable time and incredible talents to making the photographic samples in this book, and my utmost thanks to all of my students who allowed their beautiful blocks to be photographed for this book: Diana Lynn Channer, Cathy Kucenski, Dot Murdoch, Lisa Reber, Heather Semet, Pat Svitek, and Teri Weed.

My gratitude to Martingale & Company for publishing this, my fifth book for them.

Many thanks, also, to my editor, Laurie Baker, for all she has done to make this a better book.

Contents

introduction

Almost everyone who loves hand appliqué appreciates the unending sources of design in nature, from birds, butterflies, trees, and landscapes, to gardens filled with beautiful flowers. The floral blocks in this book include many of my favorite blooms, including calla lilies, anemones, irises, orchids, and more.

The blocks in this book progress from easier to more advanced, although any of them can be stitched by both beginners and expert appliquérs. (If you're a beginner, please consult one of my previous books or another reference book for the basics.) Each of the designs is made to fit a 12"-square finished block (12½" square with seam allowances). If this size is different from the size you would like to make, you can easily enlarge or reduce the designs to whatever dimensions you desire.

I hope you will also try out my new technique called "Scrapliqué," which is used in the vase of the Tulip block shown at right. In this totally free-form technique, you decide how large, how small, and what shape you would like each piece to be and the result will be a totally unique mosaic of patchwork pieces. Unit appliqué (explained on pages 10–14) allows you to create this mosaic-like pattern in any size, without ever having to hold tiny pieces together to stitch them. Check out the "Gallery of Quilts" on pages 25–35 and see how my students have used this new technique in their tulip vases and how it makes the border of Diana Lynn Channer's quilt (page 32) glow with light.

Enjoy stitching some or all of these flowers in my new collection and don't be afraid to mix elements from various blocks to create your own unique floral designs.

Jane Townswick

tools and supplies

Using the right equipment makes any quiltmaking task easier, more accurate, and more fun. Here are the tools and supplies I currently keep on hand at all times for hand appliqué. Check "Resources" on page 112 for companies that carry some of these products.

- ▶ 9½", 12", and 15" square Omnigrid rulers
- ▶ 1" x 6", 3" x 18", and 6" x 24" Omnigrid rulers
- ▶ 45 mm rotary cutter
- ▶ 24" x 36" self-healing cutting mat
- ▶ Clover silk pins
- ▶ Jeana Kimball's Foxglove Cottage extra-sharp appliqué pins
- ▶ Jeana Kimball's Foxglove Cottage size 11 straw needles
- ▶ John James size 12 Sharp needles
- ▶ YLI's 100-denier silk thread, in colors 226, 235, 239, 242, and the coral color 217
- ▶ Natural (or bleached, cosmetic-quality) beeswax, available at craft stores, quilt shops, or beauty-supply stores
- ▶ Comfortable thimble
- ▶ 4" bamboo skewers or round wooden toothpicks with sharp tips
- ▶ 3½" Gingher embroidery scissors with a micro-serrated blade, for cutting fabric
- ▶ Scissors for cutting paper
- ▶ Avery glue pen, for glue-basting fabric
- ▶ Freezer paper, template plastic, Avery label paper, or CAT paper, for making templates. CAT paper (Clear Appliqué Template paper) is an opaque paper with an adhesive back that adheres easily to fabric.
- ▶ Sharpie black ultra-fine-point permanent marking pen, for marking templates
- ▶ Quilter's Choice silver pencil, for marking fabric
- ▶ Pigma .01 mm marking pens in black and in colors, for inking fabric
- ▶ Small wooden "finger-creasing" iron

unit appliqué

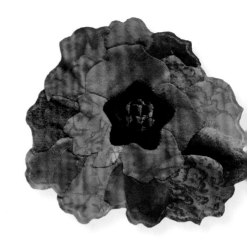

When an appliqué motif consists of two or more shapes that are positioned right next to each other, you can stitch them into a unit *before* you stitch the unit onto background fabric. Unit appliqué is great for motifs that require templates, and it can also be done with free-form cutting, without templates.

It doesn't matter whether the seams of an appliqué unit are straight or curved—as long as the pieces are connected to each other, you can stitch them into a unit. Read through the following advantages of this technique and enjoy using either free-form unit appliqué or template unit appliqué whenever they apply to projects you want to make.

ADVANTAGES

• Because you always stitch one edge of the first appliqué shape to a larger piece of fabric *before you mark the following appliqué shape on that fabric*, it is simple to make sure that there are no gaps between shapes.

• You can work with any size appliqué shape easily— even the tiniest and narrowest ones.

• It is easy to select the color you want for each successive shape, because you can lay the preceding shape on a piece of fabric and move it around until you find just the color you like for the following shape (see "Color Blending" on page 15).

• It's easier to position units on background fabric than individual shapes, especially small or narrow ones.

• It's easier to stitch completed units to the background than it is to try to make separate shapes fit together on the background one at a time.

UNIT APPLIQUÉ THAT REQUIRES TEMPLATES

Follow these steps to stitch appliqué units that require templates.

1. Using a fine-point permanent marking pen, trace the Camellia flower appliqué motif from page 55 onto the dull side of a piece of freezer paper. Include the little hatch marks that show where two shapes start or stop being joined. Roughly cut out the flower template, keeping the individual petal shapes joined. Mark the numbers of the stitching sequence on the freezer-paper petals.

2. Cut petal #1 and the center motifs from the freezer-paper template; lay them aside temporarily.

3. Press the freezer-paper template for petal #1 onto the right side of your chosen fabric and mark around it with a removable fabric-marking pen or pencil, *except* at the edge that will be covered by the center circle. Leave that area unmarked. Remember to mark the little hatch mark that shows where petal #1 will join petal #2. Remove the freezer paper.

4. Using small, sharp-to-the-tip scissors, cut out the fabric shape for petal #1, adding a 3/16" seam allowance as you go. Extend the seam allowances at the inside edge of petal #1 to a generous 1/4", to make sure that the center circle will cover the petal with no gaps. Clip the hatch mark up to, but not through, the marked turning line.

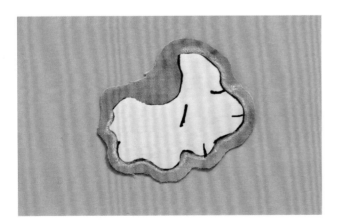

5. Decide what color fabric you would like to use for petal #2. Appliqué the upper-right edge of petal #1 onto your chosen fabric, beginning at the top hatch mark on the right side and ending at the hatch mark where the piece meets the center motif.

6. Cut petal #2 from the freezer-paper template and press it next to the stitched line on petal #1. Mark around petal #2 with the removable fabric-marking pen or pencil.

7. Remove the freezer-paper template for petal #2 and cut a ³⁄₁₆" seam allowance around the petal #2 shape, leaving a generous ¼" seam allowance at the inside edge.

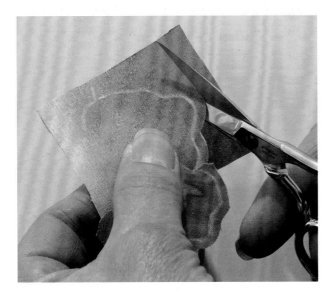

8. Lift petal #1 and cut the underlying seam allowance of petal #2 even with the seam allowance of petal #1. Petals #1 and #2 are now joined.

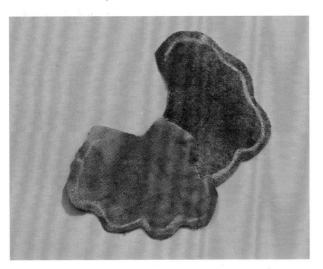

9. Appliqué the edge of petal #2 to a piece of fabric that is large enough to accommodate petal #3 and continue as before to add petal #3 to the unit.

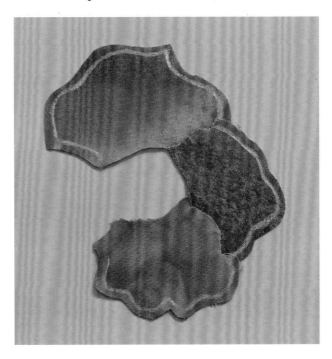

10. Continue adding petals to the growing unit in the same manner until all the petals are joined.

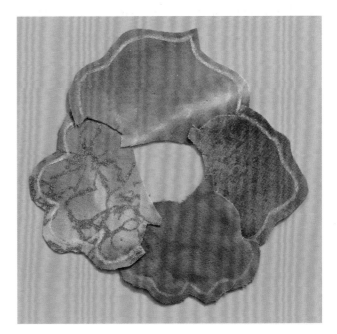

11. To find the size center circle you need, lay a circle stencil over the center circle on page 55. When you have found the matching size circle, *move up two or three sizes on the stencil and mark that size circle* on the right side of your chosen fabric. This will allow for the width of your marked line. Cut a ³⁄₁₆" seam allowance around the fabric circle and appliqué it to the center petal shape. Appliqué the center unit over the underlying flower unit.

12. Make as many appliqué units as needed for your project and arrange them on your background fabric as desired. When you are happy with your arrangement, appliqué each unit and any single shapes in place.

UNIT APPLIQUÉ THAT DOESN'T REQUIRE TEMPLATES

You can also create beautiful units by cutting individual appliqué shapes by eye. Follow these steps to create artistic, imaginative motifs like the Anemone (see page 37) without templates.

1. Begin by cutting a petal shape that is approximately 2" long and about ½" wide. As you cut, make the edges slightly uneven, for an interesting, natural look in the finished shape. Cut a curve at the "top" of this petal, and cut the "bottom" edge straight across. Make sure that the petal is slightly narrower at the bottom than at the middle and top.

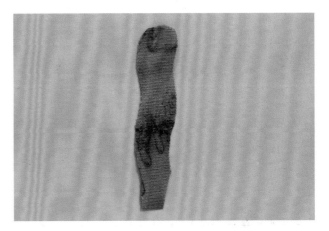

2. Along the long edges of the petal, make a few ⅛"-deep clips into the seam allowances of any areas that have inner curves. Space these clips approximately ⅛" apart. Do not clip into areas with outer curves.

3. Beginning about 3⁄16" in from the top of the petal shape, clip and appliqué the left edge to a piece of fabric that is large enough for the second petal. The fabric for the second petal should be a similar value (lightness or darkness) to the first petal (see "Color Blending" on page 15). Stitch from the top clip to the bottom of the petal. Each petal you stitch should be narrower at the bottom than at the top so that your finished flower will curve into a circle.

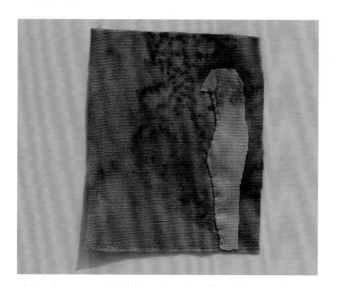

4. Cut a free-form shape from the fabric for the second petal, creating a curve at the top and a slightly uneven long edge that is approximately 3⁄8" from the stitched line. As you move toward the bottom edge, narrow the width of petal #2 slightly. Lift petal #1 up to cut the underneath seam allowance for petal #2 even with the seam allowance of petal #1.

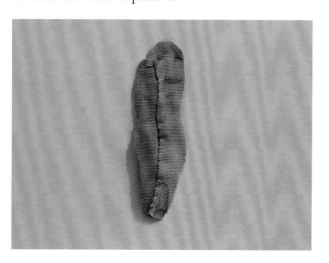

5. Continue as established, adding as many petals to the unit as you desire. Make sure that you turn under slightly more of the seam allowance as you stitch toward the bottom of each petal so that your finished flower will look natural and realistic.

color blending

You can create rich visual depth with my color-blending technique, which involves combining many different fabrics within an appliqué shape. Here are some examples and guidelines to follow as you select fabrics. After reading through them, play with some fabrics from your stash and enjoy coming up with your own color and value sequences.

Color **value** (the lightness or darkness of a color) is *more important than the color itself* for color blending fabrics for appliqué. Use similar values beside each other, and your fabrics will blend together visually, no matter what colors you choose. You can create a progression from light to dark or from dark to light.

You can also position lights in the center area and move toward darks on either side, or vice versa.

Abrupt changes in color value draw the eye to a specific area of an appliqué shape. Unless you really wish to create this particular effect (which can sometimes be a creative option), avoid sudden switches in color value.

You can mix color values within an appliqué shape to highlight certain areas, as shown in this flower. While the basic progression of similar color values is kept intact throughout the shape, lighter colors draw the eye to certain areas of the flower.

You can use small-scale multicolored prints, tone-on-tone fabrics, solids, hand-painted fabrics, batiks, or any other fabrics that please you for color blending. As long as you keep color values similar between neighboring shapes, you can create exciting visual effects.

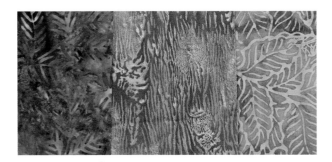

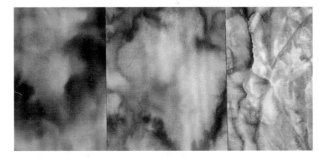

Avoid plaids or high-contrast prints for color blending. Fabrics like these draw attention to themselves, which makes them unsuitable for color blending.

special techniques

Many of the blocks in this book feature one or more special techniques I have developed for adding details, such as veins in leaves, or multipart stems and branches. Steep outer points are now as easy to stitch as wider points, and my new technique, called "scrapliqué," is great for working with uneven pieces of fabric to create a mosaic-like patchwork.

SCRAPLIQUÉ

Follow the steps below to scrapliqué the vase shown in the Tulips block (page 107). Browse through the "Gallery of Quilts" on pages 25–35 for more examples of how you can use this new technique in your work.

1. Using a small pair of sharp-to-the-tip scissors, cut a free-form shape with five straight sides from your desired fabric. This shape should measure *approximately* 1" across, so that it will be large enough to include about a 3⁄16" seam allowance on each side.

2. Select a piece of fabric in the color you would like for the second appliqué shape. This can be any color that pleases you. If you want to go for a color-blended look, keep the values similar. If you'd like to go for a high-contrast look, choose a fabric that contrasts in color value. Decide which edge of the first shape you want to stitch to the fabric for shape #2 and finger-press a 3⁄16" seam allowance along that edge. Beginning 3⁄16" in from

the right edge of the folded edge, appliqué the first cut shape to your chosen fabric for the second shape. Finish this seam 3⁄16" in from the left edge of the fabric.

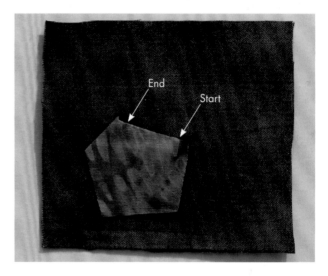

3. Cut out shape #2 free form, beginning and ending even with the stitched edge of the first shape. Cut the edges of shape #2 by eye, at the angles you like, keeping the beginning and ending points even with the edge of shape #1.

4. After you have cut shape #2, lift up shape #1 and cut the seam allowance of shape #2 even with the seam allowance of shape #1 underneath. Finger-press these seam allowances open.

5. Turn under and finger-press another ³⁄₁₆" seam allowance along two adjacent edges of shapes #1 and #2.

6. Beginning and ending ³⁄₁₆" in from each end of the fold, stitch the folded edge of shapes #1 and #2 to another piece of fabric for shape #3.

7. Cut out shape #3 free form, beginning and ending even with the edge of shape #1 and shape #2. Finger-press the seam allowances open, as before.

8. Continue adding free-form shapes until your unit is large enough to hold the template you wish to trace and cut from it. As you continue adding shapes, you can choose any edge of any shape to stitch to the next fabric. The resulting appliqué piece will resemble a mosaic of shapes or a colorful crazy quilt.

FREE-FORM STEMS AND BRANCHES

You can enhance the look of stems and branches by using two or more fabrics in them. Even a ¼"-wide stem is large enough to include two or three fabrics. Try this technique and see if you enjoy the realistic look of your work.

1. For any of the free-form stems or branches in this book, you can use the patterns given with each block, or be adventurous and stitch your own free-form shapes. To learn this technique, start by cutting a ⅜" x 4" stem with any curvature you like.

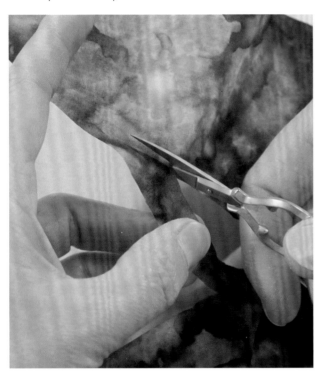

2. Appliqué one long edge of this stem to a second piece of fabric in any color you like. As you stitch, make clips into the seam allowance of the stem at different depths, so that the stitched edge will not be a straight line.

3. Cut the second fabric approximately ¼" from your stitched line.

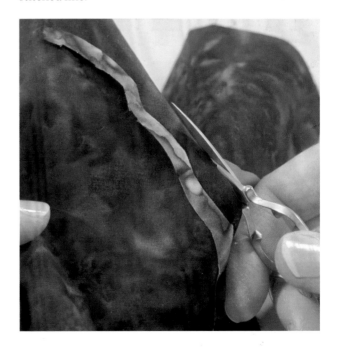

4. Lift up the first portion of the stem you stitched and trim the seam allowance of the second fabric even with the seam allowance of the first piece.

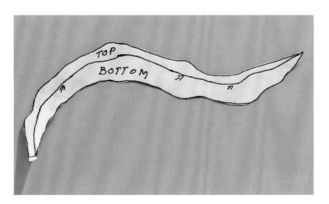

5. To add more fabrics for a wider stem or branch, repeat steps 2–4.

INSERTING A THIN BAND OF COLOR

Follow these steps to insert a narrow vein into a two-part leaf. Then look through the "Gallery of Quilts" on pages 25–35 to see more innovative ways to use this technique.

1. Using a fine-point permanent black marking pen, trace the B-1/B-2 leaf shape from the left side of the "Anemone" pattern on page 42 onto the dull side of a piece of freezer paper. Mark the letters and numbers on the templates, as shown, and cut out the leaf along the outer edges.

2. Cut the leaf template apart along the center line. Press the half marked B-1 onto the right side of your chosen fabric for this shape. Using a removable fabric-marking pen or pencil, mark around the template. Mark little arrows pointing to the edge above the B-1 label so it will be easy to remember which edge of this shape you want to appliqué. Remove the freezer-paper template and cut a 3/16" seam allowance around this lower half of the leaf.

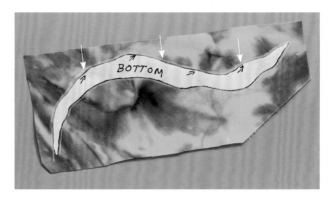

3. Appliqué the center line of the bottom leaf shape to a piece of fabric in the color you choose for the vein. This fabric can be any color you like. It must be large enough to hold the entire length of the leaf shape. Begin about ½" in from the top point and end stitching at the opposite end of the leaf.

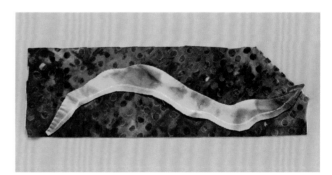

4. Cut the vein fabric approximately ¼" from your stitched line. Lift up the B-1 piece and cut the vein fabric even with the edge of the seam allowance underneath.

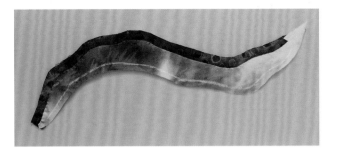

5. Turn under the vein fabric until only about ¹⁄₁₆" of it is visible next to the stitched line of the leaf. Finger-press the vein fabric along the fold, allowing it to be slightly uneven for an artistic look. Stitch the creased vein to a piece of fabric for the B-2 half of the leaf.

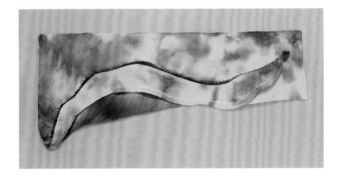

6. Press the B-2 freezer-paper template *over* the stitched vein and next to the stitched line of the B-1 half. Using a fabric-marking pen or pencil, mark around the outer edge of the B-2 template.

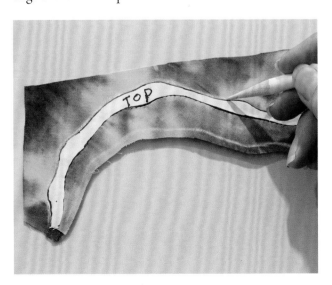

7. Remove the freezer-paper template and cut a ³⁄₁₆" seam allowance around the entire leaf shape. Lift B-1 and cut the seam allowance of B-2 even with the seam allowance of the vein.

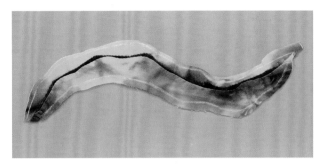

Steep Outer Points

No matter what the appliqué shape, or how many fabrics you choose for it, you can follow these steps to stitch any steep outer point with ease.

1. Cut a ³⁄₁₆" seam allowance around the shape that has a steep point.

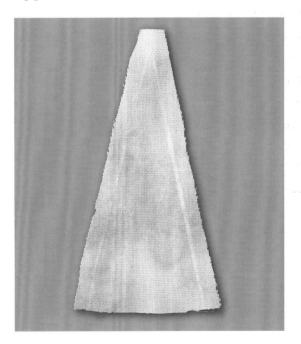

2. Appliqué the *right edge* of the appliqué shape to the background fabric all the way up to the very tip of the point. Insert the needle into the background at the very tip and bring the thread all the way through to the wrong side of your work. Take a stitch on top of your last stitch and lock the thread securely by running the needle through the circle of thread as shown.

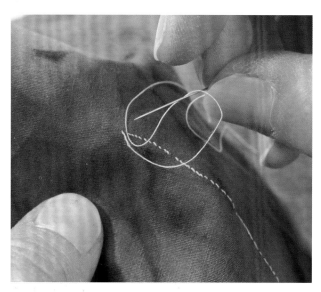

3. Clip the thread, leaving a 6" tail hanging on the wrong side of your work; you will need this thread to tie a knot after finishing the second side of the point.

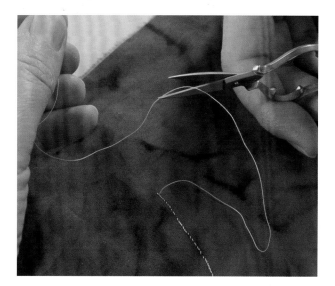

4. Clip the seam allowance on the unstitched *left* edge of the appliqué shape, approximately ½" to ¾" down from the tip of the point. Turn under and stitch the seam allowance from the clip to the end of the appliqué shape.

5. On the wrong side of your work, cut the background fabric *only*. Referring to the photo and starting approximately ¼" below the place where your stitching stops on the *unfinished* side of the appliqué shape, cut straight up to the very tip of the point. Then cut over to (but not through) the stitched line. It is helpful to mark these cutting lines before you begin.

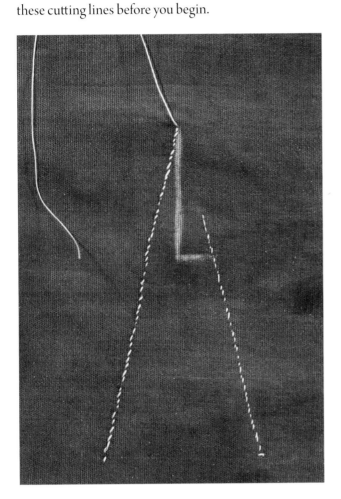

6. Using a bamboo skewer or toothpick, gently lift up the narrow L-shaped flap of background fabric and fold it over the partially stitched line.

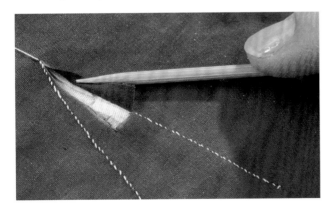

7. Press down the fabric with your finger, creating a fold that continues perfectly straight from your stitched line.

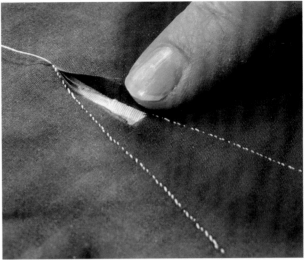

8. Continue this process until the entire L-shaped flap of fabric is creased all the way up to the tip of the point.

9. When you are happy with the way the folded edge looks, coat the tip of a bamboo skewer or toothpick with glue from a glue stick.

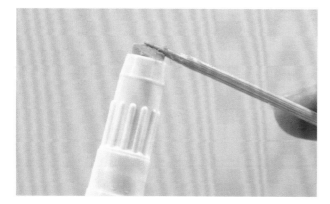

10. Run the glue underneath the fold. Then pinch the fabric in place with your finger to baste it in place.

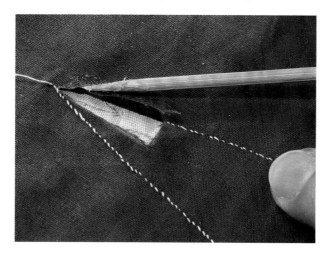

11. Pick up your work and use your left index finger to push the seam allowance of the appliqué shape all the way through to the wrong side of your work, as shown.

12. On the right side of your work, you will have a perfectly accurate, glue-basted fold at the unstitched area on the left side of the appliqué shape. Thread a needle with thread that matches your *background* fabric and stitch this short, folded edge to the appliqué shape, ending at the very tip of the steep point.

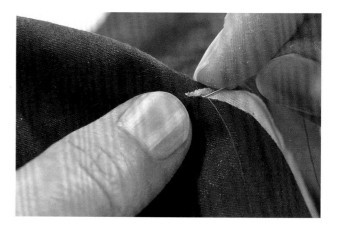

13. When you take the last stitch at the very tip of the steep point, take the needle all the way through to the wrong side of your work. Using this thread and the 6" tail of thread left hanging, tie two square knots at the tip of the steep point and clip the threads close to the knot.

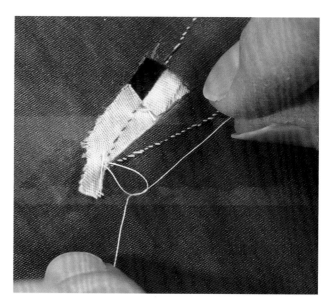

Gallery of Quilts

Check out the distinctive color palettes, lovely embellishments, and expert stitching of the talented quiltmakers from this class and bring your own imagination into play as you stitch your own quilt creations.

Tulip Fan-cy

40" x 40"

By Gayle Lynn Rosenbach, Springfield, New Jersey, January 2009

I adapted this traditional Chinese Fan pattern to display Jane's tulips using a rainbow of colors and some of my favorite Asian and Kaffe Fassett fabrics; the fans were machine appliquéd. After scouring through my extensive collection of quilting books and magazines to find the perfect setting for the tulips, imagine my surprise to discover that a similar quilt has been covering my daughter's bed for the last 20 years!

Blakesly's Garden

68" x 68"

By Patricia J. Svitek, Thornton, Pennsylvania, December 2008

This quilt is dedicated to the memory of my wonderful father who encouraged his family never to give up and to live each day to the fullest. Choosing fabrics, creating, stitching, and embellishing each block helped me through one of the saddest times of my life. While making this quilt, even a broken wrist didn't stop me from blending fabric in the color-blending method that Jane taught.

Dad created many beautiful flowers in his family, and I created this quilt to remember him. The gorgeous machine quilting was done by Lorac Designs.

It Started with the Tulips

48" x 70"

By Pam Ellenberger, Reading, Pennsylvania, January 2009

This quilt has been an adventure in stretching my skills—appliqué, color usage, piecing, and machine quilting. The classes and the beautiful creations of the other students helped keep me motivated to complete the piece.

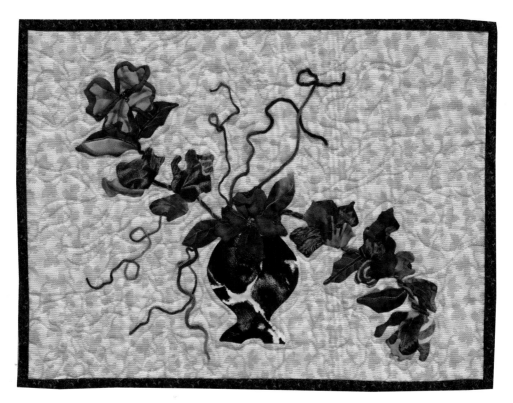

Kousa Rosa Bella

17" x 13"

By JoAnne Yarnall, West Chester, Pennsylvania, December 2007

This is the first pattern I used with nothing but a line drawing from Jane. It forced me to use my imagination with no color guidance. It took several tries to get this result, one that I am very pleased with. Special thanks to Carol Heisler of Lorac Designs for the machine quilting.

Pink Princess

16½" x 16½"

By Louise Morrow, Allentown, Pennsylvania, January 2009

When I start one of Jane's patterns, I work in anticipation of the result, and when it is done, I can't believe I actually made such an awesome flower. I feel this big "WOW" inside me. I loved doing the camellia, as it is one of my favorite flowers.

Stars and Flowers

50" x 50"

By Teri Weed, Wynnewood, Pennsylvania, January 2009

For this quilt, I wanted the appliqué blocks to look rounded. I found the perfect pattern to complement the flowers in this colorful star pattern. It makes the appliqué blocks look like they extend into the sashing strips. I used an extra block as the label for the back of the quilt.

My Friends Are My Tulips

24" x 24"

By JoAnne Yarnall, West Chester, Pennsylvania, January 2009

I looked up the meaning of the word "tulips" and found this description: "They are not too elegant, not too romantic, not too big, too small, or too bright. They are like a favorite pair of jeans or your mom's fresh-baked cookies, in that the meanings of tulips express genuine coziness and comfort in all of the right ways." This describes the friends that laugh with me and cry with me and save all those little scraps of fabric that I love to use in my appliqué projects. These tulips are set a little crooked, but so am I. Special thanks to Carol Heisler of Lorac Designs for the machine quilting.

Pretty Tulips

18¾" x 23¼"

By Dorothy Murdoch, West Chester, Pennsylvania, November 2008

I enjoy making small quilts that showcase a single appliqué block. This one-block quilt is treated differently on the top edge than it is on the bottom edge; creative colors surround the tulips and make them shine. The sequins at the flower centers make the flowers twinkle in the light, which is the effect I wanted. This piece was machine quilted by Carol Heisler of Lorac Designs.

Petals and Vines

53" x 67"

By Diana Lynn Channer, Schwenksville, Pennsylvania, February 2009

Jane has done it again with her wonderful designs! Four-strand braided bias vines twist and turn among exotic beaded blossoms in this colorful quilt. The whole garden is surrounded by a lush border in multiple shades of green. If you look closely, you'll find delicate embroidery and stray leaves hidden within the border. There's even a trace of early morning fog in the corners.

A Puzzle to the Botanist

44" x 65"

By Lisa Reber, Red Hill, Pennsylvania, January 2009

Jane's designs, teaching, and classes are always an inspiration. For this quilt, I was inspired to use more of my own hand-dyed fabrics and learn new dye techniques, as well as experiment with more varied fabrics in the blocks. The crackled vase in the tulip block was Jane's new and different scrappliqué technique, and it was wonderful to see all the different results achieved by the students in the class. Each class and design brings new revelations in the artistry of quilting and new goals to which to aspire.

Orchid Elegance

16½" x 16½"

By Louise Morrow, Allentown, Pennsylvania, January 2009

Jane has such a unique appliqué technique that looks far more complicated than it is. I enjoyed the color-blending techniques and playing with the light and dark values to bring harmony to the orchid petals. I am so pleased with the results. Thank you, Jane.

Flowers from Mary Jane's Garden

15" x 15"

By Cathy Kucenski, Sinking Spring, Pennsylvania, January 2009

These designs of Jane's remind me of the many flowers in my mother's garden when I was growing up in Ste. Genevieve, Missouri. Each month I could hardly wait to see what flower we would work in next. I've completed 6 of the 12 blocks designed by Jane, and I am looking forward to stitching the remaining blocks to finish a quilt I will call "Flowers from Mary Jane's Garden" after my mother, who passed away in December 1988.

The Blocks

Anemone

Stitched by Diana Lynn Channer

The beautiful color blending in this flower makes it shimmer with light. The individual flower petals and leaf veins are cut free form, to let each individual piece "grow" naturally from your scissors as you go.

Techniques

Unit appliqué (page 10)

Color blending (page 15)

Free-form stems and branches (page 19)

Inserting a thin band of color (page 20)

Fabrics and Supplies

▸ Wide assortment of fabric scraps in lights, mediums, and darks for flower petals. (Batiks with lots of blended colors in them are great for color blending.)

▸ 4" square of contrast-color fabric for large scalloped-flower center

▸ 2" square of contrast-color fabric for medium flower center

▸ Assortment of 2"-square fabric scraps for flower buds

▸ 3 (more, if desired for color variety) fat quarters of fabric for large and medium leaves, calyxes, and free-form stems

▸ 1 fat quarter of contrast-color fabric for leaf veins

▸ Assortment of seed beads for embellishing medium flower center

A Unit: Flower

1. Free-form cut the first petal from your desired fabric. It should be about ½" x 2½" to make sure that the large scalloped flower center will overlap the inner ends of the petal easily; the top edge should be rounded, while the bottom edge should be cut straight across. This petal will have approximately ³⁄₁₆" seam allowances on both of the long edges.

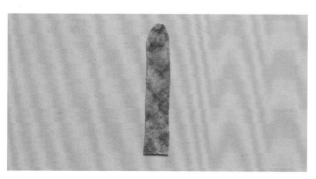

2. Turn the seam allowance under along the left edge and lay the first cut petal on the right side of the fabric selected for the second petal. Starting about ⅛" in from the top of the left edge, stitch the first petal in place on the uncut piece of fabric. As you work toward the lower edge, turn under a little more fabric for the seam allowance, so that the petal narrows. Stitch all the way to the bottom edge of the first petal.

3. Cut the second petal shape, about ⅜" x 2½", from the fabric. Lift up the first petal to cut the seam allowance of the second petal even with the seam allowance of the first petal.

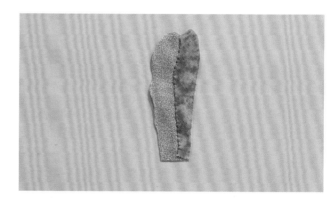

4. Continue as established, adding more and more petals and narrowing the bottom edges of each one to create a circular flower. Stitch the folded edge of the last petal to the cut edge of the first petal.

5. Appliqué the large scalloped flower center over the inner edges of the flower petals, and then add the medium flower center on top of that.

6. Embellish the medium flower center with seed beads, following the tip above right.

STITCHING BEADS IN PLACE

For longevity's sake, consider stitching each bead to your block individually, running the thread through each bead twice, taking the thread to the back of your work, and stitching a knot to hold each one in place singly. Also take a stitch or two on the wrong side of your work before moving on to sew the next bead. This does take time, but it's worth it to keep the beads in place for the entire life of your block or quilt.

B UNITS: LEAVES

1. Using a fine-point permanent black marking pen, trace the leaf shape B-1/B-2 from page 42 onto the dull side of a piece of freezer paper and include the arrow that points to the center seam, as well as the letters and numbers. Cut out the template along the outer edges, and then cut it apart along the center line. Press template B-1 onto the right side of your chosen fabric and mark around it with a fabric-marking pencil, including the arrow to remind you which edge of this shape to stitch first.

2. Remove the freezer-paper template and cut a ³⁄₁₆" seam allowance around the B-1 shape.

3. Appliqué the center seam of the B-1 piece to a piece of fabric for the vein.

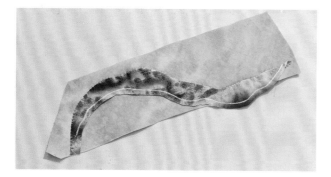

4. Cut the vein fabric approximately ¼" from your stitched line, allowing the edge to be slightly uneven as you cut. Lift up the B-1 piece to cut the seam allowance for the vein even with the seam allowance of the B-1 piece.

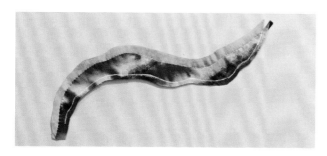

5. Turn under the vein fabric, making clips no deeper than ⅛" in the seam allowance of any areas that have inner curves. Finger-press the vein so that only about 1⁄16" is visible and stitch this creased edge to a piece of fabric that is large enough to hold the B-2 template.

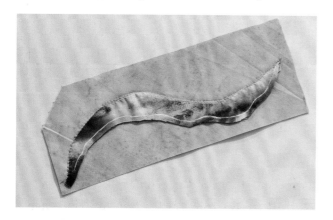

6. Press the B-2 template *over* the stitched vein, right next to your *first* stitched line. This will prevent widening out the leaf shape by the width of the vein. Mark around template B-2. Remove the freezer-paper template and cut a 3⁄16" seam allowance around shape B-2, cutting the seam allowance underneath even with the seam allowance of the vein.

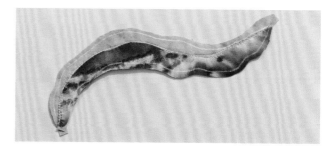

7. Continue as established to stitch the remaining leaf units that surround the flower.

C Units: Stems

1. Cut a strip of fabric on the bias that measures approximately ⅜" x 2¾", allowing the edges to be slightly uneven. Appliqué one of the long edges of this shape to a larger piece of fabric for the center portion of the stem. You can stitch this seam along the bias of the fabric or to any area of the fabric that has the color you want for the second shape.

2. Cut the larger piece of fabric to about ¼" from the stitched seam, allowing the edge to be slightly uneven. Lift up the first piece to cut the seam allowance for the second piece even with the first.

3. Turn under and finger-press the edge of the second portion of the stem. Stitch the folded edge of the second strip to a larger piece of fabric for the third portion of the stem and repeat step 2 to cut the seam allowance around it. You can finger-press the outer edges of the stem before you appliqué it to the background fabric, or crease each edge as you stitch it.

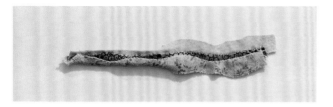

4. Repeat steps 1–3 twice more for a total of three stems.

D Units: Buds

1. Using a fine-point permanent black marking pen, trace the D-1 through D-3 bud from page 43 onto the dull side of a piece of freezer paper, including the hatch marks that show where the D-1 center piece touches pieces D-2 and D-3. Cut out the bud template along the outer edges; then cut the three pieces apart. Press template D-1 onto the right side of your chosen fabric. Mark around it, including the hatch marks.

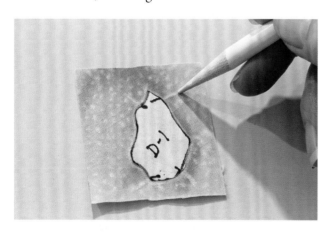

2. Remove the freezer-paper template and cut a ³⁄₁₆" seam allowance around the D-1 shape. Clip the seam allowance at the two hatch marks. Beginning at the

hatch mark at the top and ending at the hatch mark at the bottom, appliqué the left edge of the D-1 shape to a piece of fabric that is large enough to hold shape D-2.

3. Press the D-2 template next to this stitched line and mark around it. Remove the freezer-paper template and cut a ³⁄₁₆" seam allowance around shape D-2.

4. Continue as established to add shape D-3 to the bud.

5. Complete the remaining bud units in the same manner.

Putting It All Together

Refer to the photo on page 37 to arrange and stitch your completed units and pieces to the background fabric in the following order: leaf units, stem units, flower unit, calyx pieces at the top of the stems (these are stitched in place individually), and the bud units.

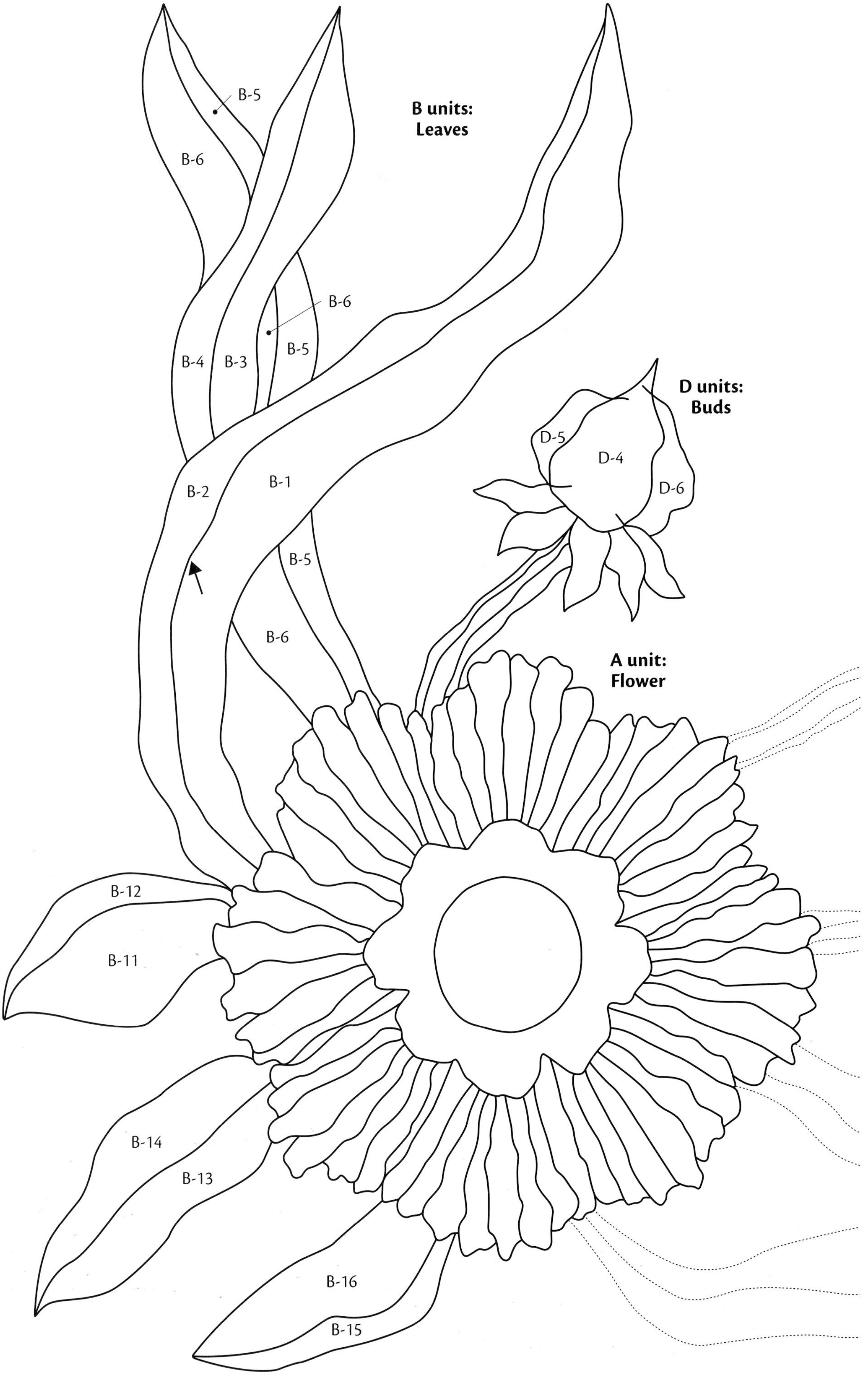

B-5

B-6

**B units:
Leaves**

B-6

B-4 B-3 B-5

B-2 B-1

**D units:
Buds**

D-5 D-4 D-6

B-5

B-6

**A unit:
Flower**

B-12

B-11

B-14

B-13

B-16

B-15

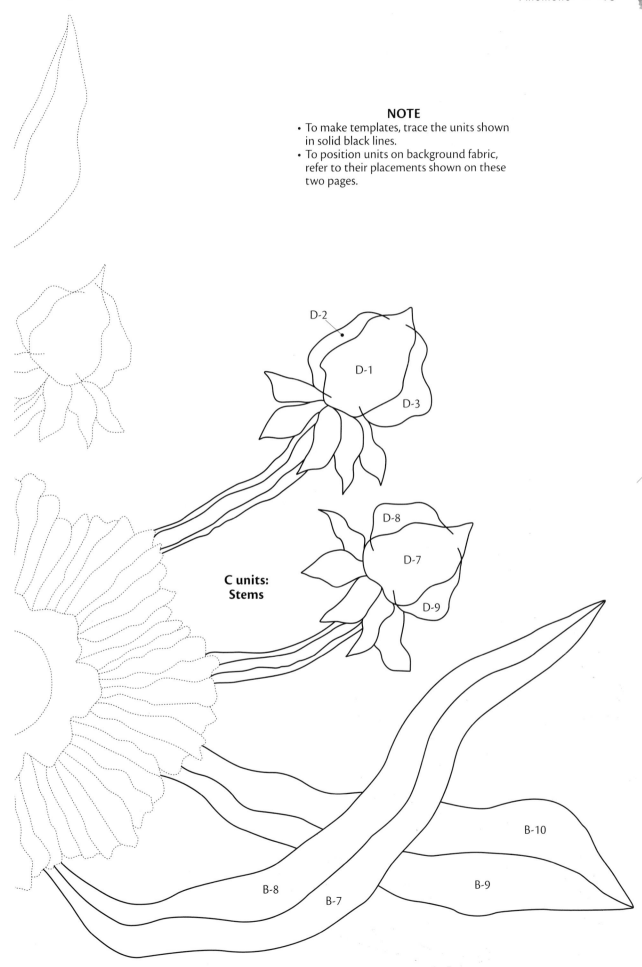

NOTE
- To make templates, trace the units shown in solid black lines.
- To position units on background fabric, refer to their placements shown on these two pages.

D-2

D-1

D-3

D-8

D-7

D-9

**C units:
Stems**

B-10

B-8

B-7

B-9

Calla Lilies

Stitched by Teri Weed

The sinuous lines of the calla lily have made it one of my longtime favorites. Here, the flower bases curve gracefully around the color-blended tops. Choose your favorite colors for these blossoms and create your own one-of-a-kind flowers.

TECHNIQUES

Unit appliqué (page 10)

Color blending (page 15)

Free-form stems and branches (page 19)

FABRICS AND SUPPLIES

▸ Wide assortment of 6" squares or scraps of fabrics for flower petals

▸ Assorted 3" squares or scraps of fabrics for stamens

▸ 3 squares, 7", or scraps of fabric for flower bases

▸ 2 or 3 fat quarters of fabric for stems, leaves, and calyxes (or see-through beads for calyxes, if desired)

A UNITS: FLOWER TOPS

1. Using a fine-point permanent black marking pen, trace the A-1 through A-12 middle flower-top unit and C-1 and C-2 flower-base unit from page 49 as one onto the dull side of a piece of freezer paper, including the letter and number on each piece. Extend the lines of the piece under the stamen (A-7) to meet the top edge of the flower base, ignoring the stamen piece temporarily. Cut out the entire template along the outer edges. Cut unit A and unit C apart along the top edge of unit C.

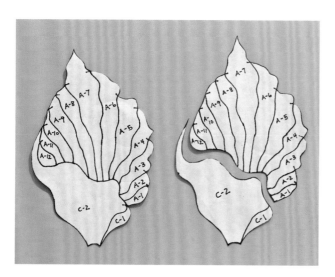

2. Working with unit A only, cut piece A-1 from the template and press it onto the right side of your chosen fabric. Mark around the A-1 template with a removable fabric-marking pencil. Remove the freezer-paper template and cut a ³⁄₁₆" seam allowance around the shape.

3. Appliqué the top edge of piece A-1 to a piece of fabric that is large enough to hold piece A-2.

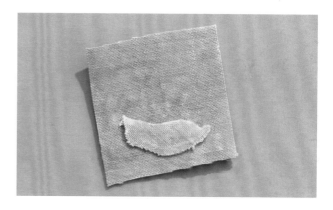

4. Cut shape A-2 from the freezer-paper template and press it next to your stitched line on the larger piece of fabric. Mark around the edges of A-2.

5. Remove the A-2 freezer-paper template and cut a ³⁄₁₆" seam allowance around the marked shape. Clip the seam allowance at the hatch mark. Lift up piece A-1 and cut the remaining portion of seam allowance even with the seam allowance of piece A-1.

6. Continue as established, adding pieces A-3 through A-12 to complete the middle flower-top unit.

7. Using the same process as for the middle flower-top unit, stitch the flower-top units at left and right in the block.

B Units: Stamens

Following the numbered stitching sequence on the middle flower-stamen unit on page 49, stitch the stamen unit in the same manner as you did the flower-top unit. Repeat for the stamens on the left and right flower-top units.

C Units: Flower Bases

1. Following the numbered stitching sequence on the middle flower base, stitch the two-part flower base in the same manner as you did the flower-top and flower-stamen units.

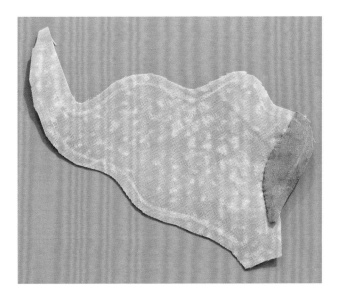

2. Using a fine-point permanent black marking pen, trace the C-3 and C-4 flower bases onto the dull side of a piece of freezer paper and cut them out. Press these templates onto your chosen fabrics. Mark around the templates, remove the freezer paper, and cut a ³⁄₁₆" seam allowance around each flower base.

D Units: Stems

1. Cut a strip of fabric on the bias that measures approximately ⅜" x 7". Appliqué one long edge of this strip to a larger piece of fabric for the center portion of the stem. Make clips randomly at different depths into the seam allowance, so that you can stitch this edge slightly unevenly.

2. Cut the larger piece of fabric to about ¼" from the stitched seam. Lift up the edge of the first strip to cut the remaining portion of seam allowance underneath even with the seam allowance of the first piece.

3. Make short clips into the second strip wherever there are any areas that have inner curves. Turn under a seam allowance along this edge and stitch the second strip to a larger piece of fabric for the third portion of the stem. Repeat step 2 to complete the stem.

4. Repeat steps 1–3 to make a total of three free-form stems, each about the same length. The edges of each stem can be trimmed as needed when you stitch them in place on the background fabric.

E Units: Leaves

1. Using a fine-point permanent black marking pen, trace the E-1/E-2 leaf shape from page 48 onto the dull side of a piece of freezer paper, including the letters and numbers. Cut out the template along the outer edges, and then cut it apart along the center line. Press template E-1 onto the right side of your chosen fabric and mark around it. Remove the freezer-paper template and cut a ³⁄₁₆" seam allowance around the E-1 shape. Stitch piece E-1 to another piece of fabric that is large enough to hold piece E-2.

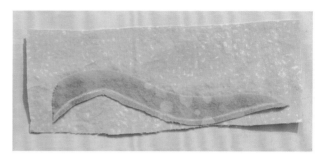

2. Press the E-2 template next to your stitched line and mark around it. Remove the freezer-paper template and cut a ³⁄₁₆" seam allowance around the E-2 shape, lifting up piece E-1 to cut the seam allowance underneath even with the seam allowance of E-1.

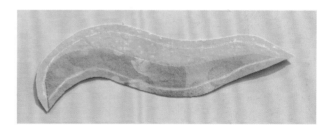

3. Continue as established to make the remaining two leaf units.

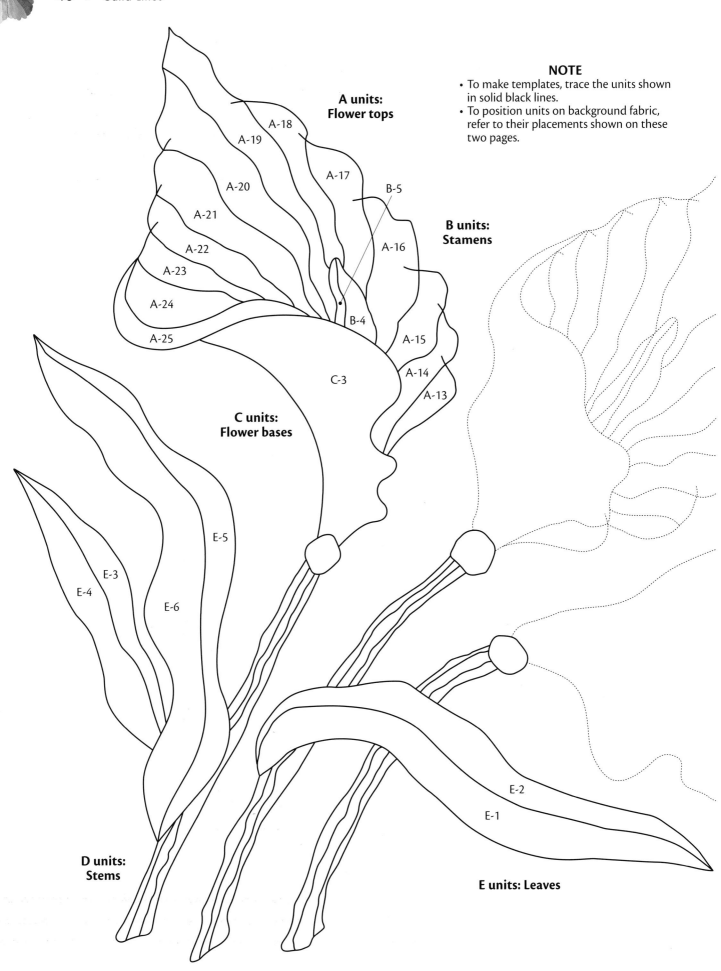

A units:
Flower tops

A-18

A-19

A-20

A-21

A-22

A-23

A-24

A-25

A-17

B-5

A-16

B units:
Stamens

B-4

A-15

A-14

A-13

C-3

C units:
Flower bases

E-5

E-3

E-4

E-6

D units:
Stems

E-2

E-1

E units: Leaves

NOTE
• To make templates, trace the units shown in solid black lines.
• To position units on background fabric, refer to their placements shown on these two pages.

CALYXES

Mark and cut out the three calyxes as individual pieces and lay them aside temporarily until you are ready to stitch them to the point where the stems and flower bases join.

PUTTING IT ALL TOGETHER

Refer to the photo on page 44 to arrange and appliqué your completed units and pieces to the background fabric in the following order: stem units, stamen units to the flower-top units, flower-base units to the flower-top units, completed flower units over the top of the stem units, calyxes over the stem-top and flower-base units, and last, the leaf units.

Camellia

Stitched by Jane Townswick

To enhance the fabrics in this flower, I started with mostly yellow prints and shaded them with pinks and oranges to create a blended yet layered look in the petals.

TECHNIQUES

Unit appliqué (page 10)

Color blending (page 15)

Free-form stems and branches (page 19)

Inserting a thin band of color (page 20)

FABRICS AND SUPPLIES

▶ Wide assortment of 4" squares or fat quarters of fabric for flower, buds, and flower center

▶ Assorted 6" squares or fat quarters of fabric for leaves, leaf veins, and stems

▶ Assorted sizes and colors of beads for flower centers (optional)

A UNIT: FLOWER

1. Trace the entire flower pattern from page 55 onto the dull side of a piece of freezer paper using a fine-point permanent black marking pen. Mark the letters, numbers, and hatch marks on each piece. Cut out the entire flower template along the outer edges. Cut piece A-5 from the template and press it onto the right side of your chosen fabric. Mark around the A-5 freezer-paper template with a fabric-marking pencil. Remove the freezer-paper template and cut a ¼" seam allowance along the top edge, so that there will be enough fabric for underlapping pieces A-12 and A-15, and a ³⁄₁₆" seam allowance around the remaining edges of piece A-5. Clip the seam allowance at the hatch marks. Beginning at the right hatch mark, appliqué the right edge of piece A-5 to a piece of fabric that is large enough to hold piece A-6.

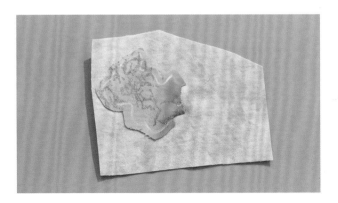

2. Cut piece A-6 from the freezer-paper template and press it next to the stitched line of piece A-5. Mark around the A-5 template, including the hatch mark. Remove the freezer paper and cut a ³⁄₁₆" seam allowance around piece A-6, making the seam allowance at the top edge about ¼" so it will underlap piece A-1 easily. Lift up piece A-5 to cut the seam allowance of piece A-6 even with the seam allowance of piece A-5. Clip the seam allowance at the hatch mark on piece A-6.

3. Continue as established, adding petals A-7 through A-15. Always remember to add the extra ¼" seam allowance at the inner edge of each piece in this unit so that the next unit will overlap the inner edges of these pieces easily.

4. Stitch together the middle unit of petals A-1 through A-4 using the same process for stitching the outer unit of petals.

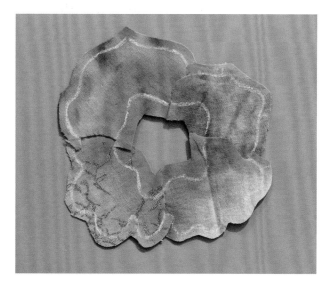

5. Mark, cut, and stitch piece A-16 onto a piece of fabric large enough for piece A-17. Cut piece A-17 from the freezer-paper template and cut out the circle. Press the template for A-17 around the stitched circle and mark around it with a fabric-marking pencil, including the hatch marks. Remove the freezer paper and cut a 3⁄16" seam allowance around piece A-17.

6. Appliqué the A-16/A-17 unit over the A-1 through A-4 petal unit. Appliqué this unit to the A-5 through A-15 petal unit.

B Units: Buds

1. Using a fine-point permanent black marking pen, trace pieces B-1 through B-3 on page 55 onto the dull side of a piece of freezer paper and cut them out. Following the same unit appliqué process as for the flower, stitch the B-1 and B-2 bud pieces together. Stitch the B-3 calyx piece over the B-1/B-2 unit.

2. Repeat the unit appliqué process to stitch the right bud unit, consisting of pieces B-4 through B-8.

C Units: Stems

1. Cut a strip of fabric on the bias that measures approximately ⅜" x 9". Appliqué one long edge of this strip to another fabric for the second portion of the stem. Make clips randomly at different depths into the seam allowance as you go, so that you can stitch this edge slightly unevenly.

2. Cut the larger piece of fabric to about ¼" from your stitched edge. Lift up the edge of the first strip to cut the seam allowance of the second strip even with the seam allowance of the first strip.

3. Make short clips into the seam allowance of the second strip wherever there are any areas that have inner curves. Turn under a seam allowance along this edge and stitch the second strip to a larger piece of fabric for the third portion of the stem. Cut the third fabric to ¼" from the stitched line and trim the seam allowance underneath as before.

4. Repeat steps 2 and 3 to add two more fabrics to the stem. Cut a 2" length from this stem for the left bud and a 1" length for the right bud and set them aside until you are ready to stitch the block together.

D Units: Leaves

1. Using a fine-point permanent black marking pen, trace leaf shape D-1/D-2 from page 55 onto the dull side of a piece of freezer paper, including the letters and numbers. Cut out the template along the outer edges, and then cut it apart along the center line. Press template D-1 onto the right side of your chosen fabric and mark around it using a removable fabric-marking pencil.

2. Remove the freezer-paper template and cut a ³⁄₁₆" seam allowance around the D-1 fabric shape.

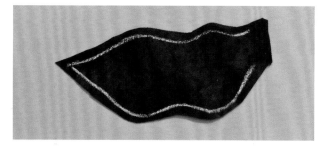

3. Appliqué the center seam of the D-1 piece to a larger piece of fabric for the vein.

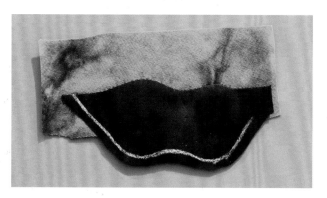

4. Cut the vein fabric to approximately ¼" from your stitched seam, allowing the edge to be slightly uneven as you cut. Lift up the D-1 piece to cut the seam allowance for the vein even with the seam allowance of the D-1 piece.

5. Turn under the seam allowance of the vein fabric and make clips no deeper than ⅛" into the seam allowance of any areas that have inner curves. Finger-press the vein, so that only about ¹⁄₁₆" is visible, and stitch this creased

edge to a piece of fabric that is large enough to hold the D-2 template.

6. Press the D-2 template *over* the stitched vein, right next to your *first* stitched line. This will avoid widening out the leaf shape by the width of the vein. Mark around template D-2. Remove the freezer paper and cut a ³⁄₁₆" seam allowance around the D-2 shape, lifting the D-1 shape and cutting the seam allowance underneath even with the seam allowance of the vein as before.

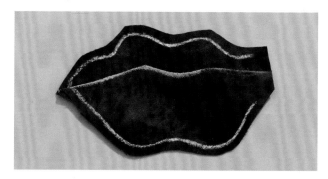

7. Continue as established to complete the remaining leaf units.

PUTTING IT ALL TOGETHER

Refer to the photo on page 50 to arrange and stitch your completed units to the background fabric in the following order: stem units, leaf units, camellia unit, and bud units. If desired, stitch the beads to the center of the large flower and the right-hand bud, referring to the tip on page 39.

NOTE
- To make templates, trace the units shown in solid black lines.
- To position units on background fabric, refer to their placements shown on pages 55 and 56.

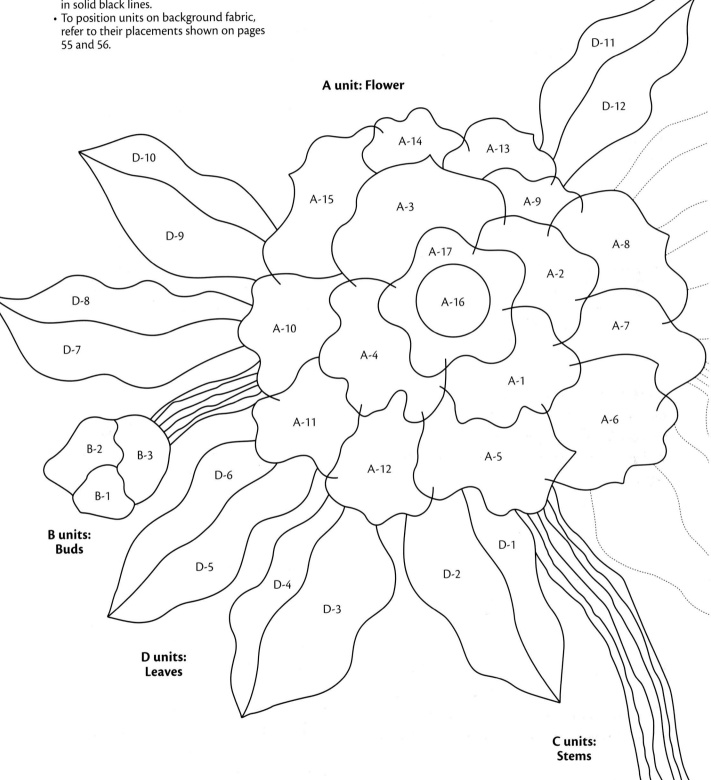

A unit: Flower

D-11
D-12
D-10
D-9
D-8
D-7
A-14
A-13
A-15
A-3
A-9
A-17
A-8
A-2
A-16
A-7
A-10
A-4
A-1
A-6
A-11
A-5
B-2
B-3
B-1
D-6
A-12
B units: Buds
D-5
D-4
D-3
D-1
D-2
D units: Leaves
C units: Stems

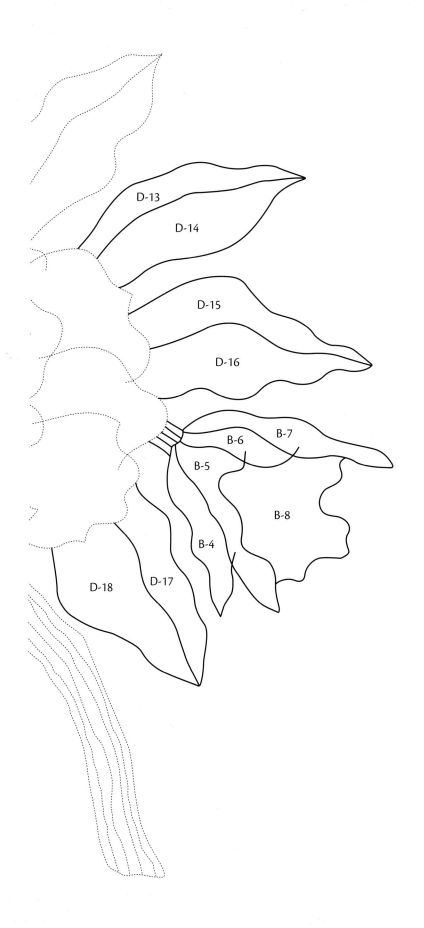

Crown Imperial

Stitched by Lisa Reber

Here's the perfect place to color blend fabrics to great effect. Notice the diversity of colors in this flower, including orangish reds, brownish reds, ochre, rust, and medium to deep purples and pinks.

TECHNIQUES

Unit appliqué (page 10)

Color blending (page 15)

Free-form stems and branches (page 19)

Inserting a thin band of color (page 20)

Steep outer points (page 21)

FABRICS AND SUPPLIES

▸ Wide assortment of 8" squares or fabric scraps for flower and stamens

▸ 3 fat quarters of fabric for stem and leaves

▸ 1 fat quarter of fabric for leaf veins

▸ Assorted sizes and colors of beads (optional)

A UNIT: FLOWER

1. Using a fine-point permanent black marking pen, trace the flower unit from page 61 onto the dull side of a piece of freezer paper and cut it out along the outer edges. Cut template A-1 from the flower-unit template and press it onto the right side of your chosen fabric. Using a removable fabric-marking pencil, mark around the A-1 template. Be sure to mark the hatch marks in the seam allowance. Cut a ³⁄₁₆" seam allowance around the A-1 shape, and remove the freezer-paper template.

2. Clip the seam allowance at the hatch marks on the left edge of piece A-1. Appliqué the left edge of piece A-1, between the hatch marks, to a piece of fabric that is large enough to hold piece A-2.

3. Cut the A-2 template from the freezer paper and press it next to your stitched line on piece A-1. Mark around piece A-2. Remove the freezer paper and cut a ³⁄₁₆" seam allowance around piece A-2, lifting up piece A-1 to cut the seam allowance of A-2 even with the seam allowance of A-1.

4. Continue as established, adding pieces A-3 through A-15.

STAMENS

The three stamens for this block are cut and stitched as single pieces. Using a fine-point permanent black marking pen, trace each one from page 61 onto the dull side of a piece of freezer paper, cut them out, and press them onto the right side of your chosen fabrics. Mark around each template, omitting the stem ends so you can lengthen them for enough underlap later before you stitch the flower unit over them.

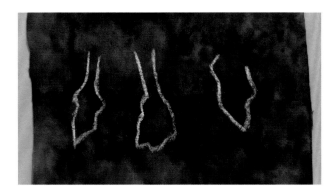

B UNIT: STEM

1. Cut a strip of fabric on the bias that measures approximately ⅜" x 7". Appliqué one long edge of this strip to another piece of fabric for the center portion of the stem. Make clips randomly, at different depths into the seam allowance, so that you can stitch this edge unevenly, for an artistic look.

2. Cut the larger piece of fabric to about ¼" from the stitched seam. Lift up the edge of the first strip to cut the seam allowance of the second piece even with the seam allowance of the first.

3. Make ⅛"-deep clips into the second strip wherever there are any areas that have inner curves. Turn under and finger-press a seam allowance along this edge and stitch the second part of the stem to a larger piece of fabric for the third portion of the stem. Repeat step 2 to complete the three-part stem.

C UNITS: LEAVES

1. Using a fine-point permanent black marking pen, trace the C-1/C-2 leaf from page 61 onto the dull side of a piece of freezer paper, including the letters and numbers. Cut out the template along the outer edges, and then cut it apart along the center line. Press piece C-1 onto the right side of your chosen fabric and mark around it. Remove the freezer-paper template and cut out piece C-1 with a ³⁄₁₆" seam allowance. Appliqué the center edge of piece C-1 to another piece of fabric that is large enough to hold the vein.

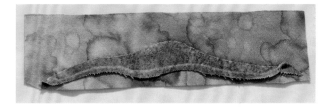

2. Cut the vein fabric ¼" from your stitched line. Lift up the C-1 piece to cut the seam allowance underneath even with the seam allowance of C-1.

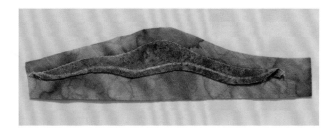

3. Make ⅛" clips into the vein fabric anywhere there are inner curves. Using your fingers, turn under and crease the vein fabric, so that only about ¹⁄₁₆" of it is visible and stitch this fold to a piece of fabric that is large enough to hold piece C-2.

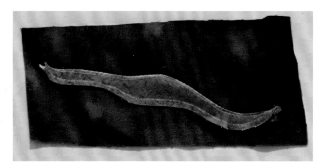

4. Press the C-2 template next to your *first* stitched line, covering the vein, so that you will not increase the width of the leaf by the width of the vein. Mark around the C-2 template with a fabric-marking pencil. Remove the freezer paper and cut a ³⁄₁₆" seam allowance around the C-2 shape, lifting up piece C-1 to cut the seam allowance of C-2 even with the seam allowance of the vein.

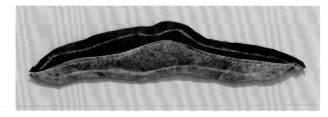

5. Continue as established to stitch the remaining leaf units.

Putting It All Together

Refer to the photo on page 57 to arrange and stitch your completed units and pieces to the background fabric in the following order, referring to "Steep Outer Points" on page 21 for the leaf units: stem unit and lower leaf units, followed by stamens, upper leaf units, and flower unit.

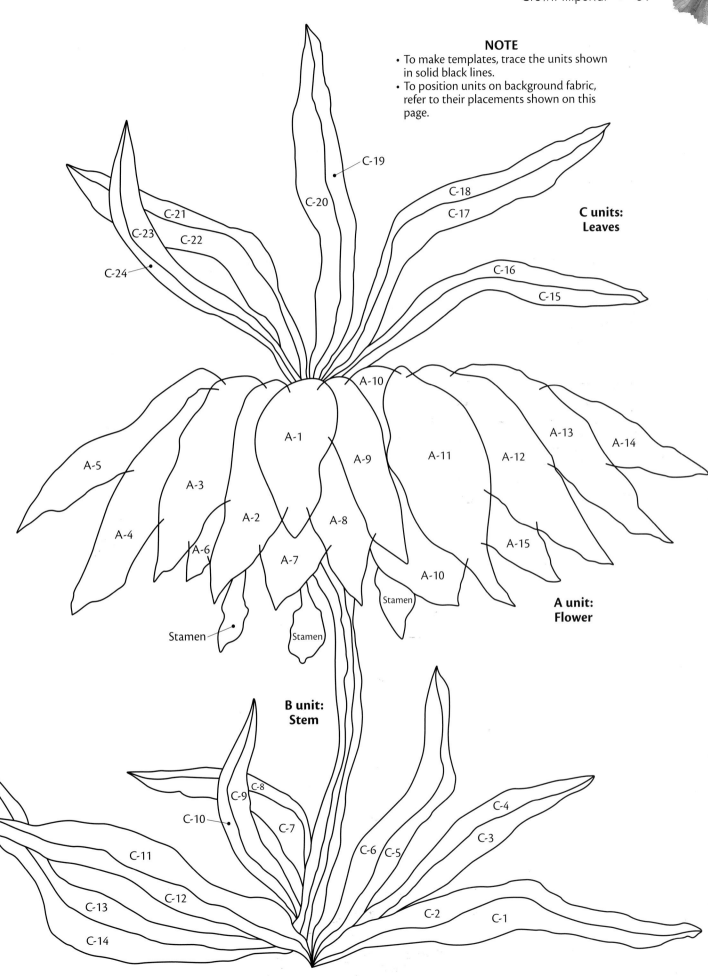

NOTE
- To make templates, trace the units shown in solid black lines.
- To position units on background fabric, refer to their placements shown on this page.

C units: Leaves

A unit: Flower

B unit: Stem

Dogwoods

Stitched by Heather Semet

Color blending in tints and tones of white gives these dogwood blossoms the look of their real counterparts. You can color-blend your own Dogwood blossoms in this same way by following the inner lines of each petal on pages 66 and 67, or cut the larger petal shapes on the solid black lines, without color blending the smaller pieces, as described in the instructions at right.

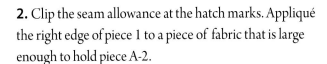

TECHNIQUES

Unit appliqué (page 10)

Color blending (page 15)

Inserting a thin band of color (page 20)

FABRICS AND SUPPLIES

▸ Wide assortment of 6" squares or scraps of fabrics for flowers

▸ 10" square of contrast-color fabric for flower tips

▸ 3 (or more, if desired) squares, 10", or scraps of fabrics for leaves

▸ 8" square of fabric for vase

▸ 8" square of contrast fabric for underneath layer of teardrop shapes on vase

▸ Decorative yarn or embroidery fibers for stems and tendrils

▸ 100-denier silk thread to match or blend with decorative yarn or embroidery fibers

▸ Assorted colors of seed beads for two flower centers

A UNITS: DOGWOOD BLOSSOMS

1. Using a fine-point permanent marking pen, trace the center flower, petals A-1 through A-4 from page 67 onto the dull side of a piece of freezer paper, including all the hatch marks (and individual numbered pieces within each petal, if desired). There is no need to mark the shaded areas at the tips of the flower. Cut the flower unit from the freezer paper along the outer edges. Cut piece A-1 from the freezer paper and press it onto the right side of your chosen fabric. Using a fabric-marking pencil, mark around piece 1, including the hatch marks. Remove the freezer-paper template and cut a ³⁄₁₆" seam allowance around this piece.

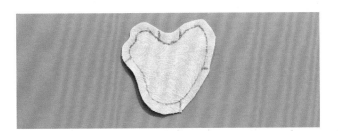

2. Clip the seam allowance at the hatch marks. Appliqué the right edge of piece 1 to a piece of fabric that is large enough to hold piece A-2.

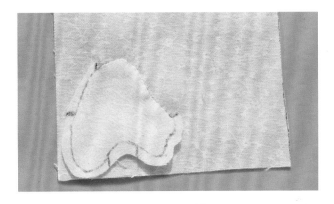

3. Cut piece A-2 from the freezer paper and press it next to your stitched line. Using a fabric-marking pencil, mark around piece A-2, including the hatch marks. Remove the freezer-paper template and cut a ³⁄₁₆" seam allowance around piece A-2, lifting up piece A-1 to cut the seam allowance underneath even with the seam allowance of piece A-1. Clip the seam allowance at the hatch marks.

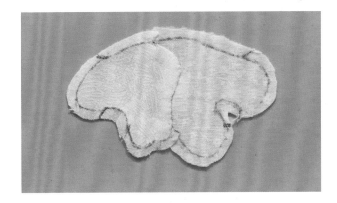

4. Add petals A-3/A-4 to the A-1/A-2 center blossom unit. Stitch the petals together using the same process. Appliqué the tips of each petal to a lower layer of contrast fabric, starting and ending at the hatch marks. Cut the contrast fabric to approximately ³⁄₁₆" from the indentation on the flower petal. These edges will be turned under as you stitch each flower unit to the background fabric, leaving a little bit of contrast color visible at each flower tip.

5. Repeat the process used to make the first blossom to make each of the remaining blossom units.

B UNITS: LEAVES

1. Using a fine-point permanent marking pen, trace the B-1/B-2 leaf shape from page 67 onto the dull side of a piece of freezer paper, including the letters and numbers. Cut out the template along the outer edges, and then cut it apart along the center line. Press piece B-1 onto the right side of your chosen fabric and mark around it. Remove the freezer-paper template and cut out piece B-1 with a ³⁄₁₆" seam allowance. Appliqué the center edge of piece B-1 to another piece of fabric that is large enough to hold the vein.

2. Cut the vein fabric ¼" from your stitched line and lift up piece B-1 to cut the seam allowance of the vein even with the seam allowance of piece B-1.

3. Make ⅛" clips into the seam allowance of the vein fabric anywhere there are inner curves. Turn under and finger-press the vein fabric, so that only about ¹⁄₁₆" of it is visible; stitch this fold to a piece of fabric that is large enough to hold piece B-2.

4. Press the B-2 template right next to your *first* stitched line, covering the vein so that you will not increase the width of the leaf by the width of the vein. Mark around the B-2 template with a fabric-marking pencil. Remove the freezer-paper template and cut a ³⁄₁₆" seam allowance around shape B-2, lifting up piece B-1 to cut the seam allowance of B-2 even with the seam allowance of the vein.

5. Continue as established to stitch the remaining leaf units.

C Unit: Vase

1. Using a fine-point permanent black marking pen, trace the C-1 vase shape from page 67 onto the dull side of a piece of freezer paper, including the inner elongated teardrop shapes. Cut out the vase along the outer edges, and cut out each teardrop shape. Press the vase template onto the right side of your chosen vase fabric; mark around the outer edges of the vase and mark *inside* each teardrop shape. Remove the freezer-paper template and cut a ³⁄₁₆" seam allowance around the outer edges of the C-1 shape.

2. Layer the vase shape on top of the 6" square of contrast fabric and insert straight pins at the four corners to hold the layers together. Cut an approximately ⅛" to ³⁄₁₆" seam allowance *inside* each inner shape, cutting through the vase fabric only. Clip the seam allowance along the curve at the top of the shape and clip to the inner point at the bottom. Turn under the seam allowance and reverse appliqué each shape to the lower layer of fabric. Repeat for each shape and add the small contrast-color shape at the bottom edge of the vase.

Tendrils and Stems

1. Using a fabric-marking pencil, mark each of the stem and tendril lines from pages 66 and 67 onto your background fabric. Knot the end of the silk thread that matches or blends with your chosen yarn or fiber. Bring the thread up from the wrong side of the background fabric to the right side, just at the start of a tendril or stem line. Place the yarn on the line and turn under the end so that no raw edge is visible. Take a stitch or two over the yarn to secure the end in place.

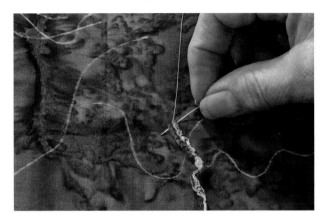

2. Take the needle to the wrong side of your work again and bring it up on the left side of the yarn, approximately ¼" from the last stitch. Take a stitch over the yarn and insert the needle into the background fabric on the opposite side of the yarn. Continue attaching the yarn in the same way until you come near the end of the marked line. If the yarn end will *not* be overlapped by an appliqué piece, fold the end of the yarn under and stitch it in place, as you did at the beginning. Stitch all the remaining stems and tendrils in the same manner.

PUTTING IT ALL TOGETHER

Refer to the photo on page 62 to arrange and stitch your completed units and pieces to the background fabric in the following order: vase unit, leaf units, and blossom units. If desired, stitch beads to the center of selected blossoms, referring to the tip on page 39.

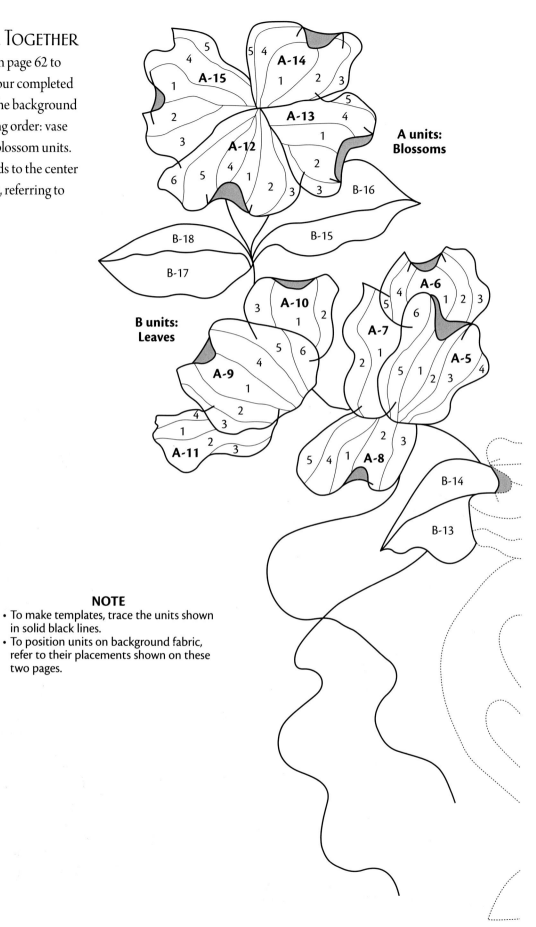

A units: Blossoms

B units: Leaves

NOTE
- To make templates, trace the units shown in solid black lines.
- To position units on background fabric, refer to their placements shown on these two pages.

C unit:
Vase

Iridaceae

Stitched by Dot Murdoch

The curvy petals of this flower seem to be lifting gently on a soft breeze. These pale petals look great on a dark background, but you could also stitch dark petals on a light background.

TECHNIQUES

Unit appliqué (page 10)

Free-form stems and branches (page 19)

Inserting a thin band of color (page 20)

FABRICS AND SUPPLIES

▶ Assorted fat quarters of fabric or scrap fabrics for flower petals

▶ 3 or more fat quarters of assorted fabrics for stems, leaves, and leaf veins

▶ 8" square or large scraps of fabric for large and small center petals

▶ 3" square of fabric for oval center motif

▶ Assorted seed beads or other decorative beads for flower center

A UNITS: OUTER PETALS

1. Using a fine-point permanent black marking pen, trace petal A-1/A-2 from page 72 onto the dull side of a piece of freezer paper, marking the center line all the way to the bottom of the petal. Cut out the petal along the outer edges, and then cut the petal apart along the center vein line. Press the A-1 template onto your chosen fabric and mark around it with a fabric-marking pencil. Remove the freezer paper and cut a ³⁄₁₆" seam allowance around it. Appliqué shape A-1 along the center line to a piece of fabric that is large enough to hold shape A-2.

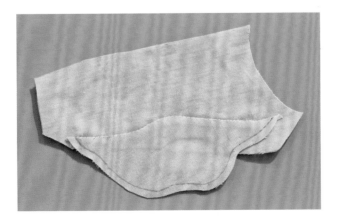

2. Press the A-2 template next to your stitched line and mark around it. Remove the freezer-paper template and cut a ³⁄₁₆" seam allowance around shape A-2, lifting up the A-1 shape to cut the seam allowance of A-2 even with the seam allowance of A-1.

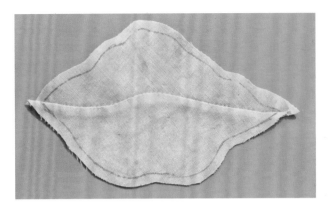

3. Continue as established for each of the remaining five large flower petals. On petal unit A-7/A-8, create the shaded area by turning the seam allowance under between the hatch marks and stitching the A-7 petal to a piece of contrast fabric. Cut a ³⁄₁₆" seam allowance on the contrast fabric.

B UNITS: STEMS WITH LEAVES

1. Using a fine-point permanent black marking pen, trace the B-1 through B-3 leaf shape from page 73 onto the dull side of a piece of freezer paper. Be sure to include the two little hatch marks on this template, indicating where shapes B-2 and B-3 touch the B-1 shape. Cut out the template along the outer edges; then cut shapes B-2 and B-3 from the template. Press the B-1 template onto the right side of your chosen fabric and mark around it with a fabric-marking pencil, including the hatch marks.

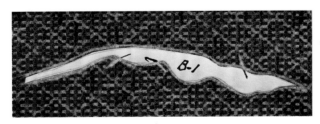

2. Remove the freezer-paper template and cut a ³⁄₁₆" seam allowance around the B-1 shape. Clip the seam allowance at the two hatch marks. Turn under the seam allowance closest to the tip of the leaf and stitch shape B-1 from the hatch mark to the bottom of the stem onto a piece of fabric that is large enough to hold shape B-2.

3. Press template B-2 next to your stitched line. Mark around it with a fabric-marking pencil. Remove the freezer-paper template and cut a ³⁄₁₆" seam allowance around shape B-2, lifting up piece B-1 to cut the seam allowance underneath even with the seam allowance of B-1. Repeat to add piece B-3.

4. Continue as established for leaf shapes B-4 through B-8.

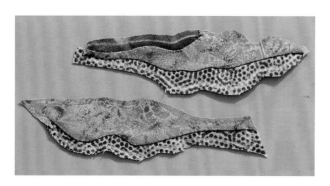

C Units: Leaves

1. Using a fine-point permanent black marking pen, trace the C-1/C-2 leaf from page 72 onto the dull side of a piece of freezer paper. Cut out the template along the outer edges, and then cut it apart along the center line. Press shape C-1 onto the right side of your chosen fabric and mark around it with a fabric-marking pencil. Remove the freezer-paper template and cut out shape C-1 with a ³⁄₁₆" seam allowance around it.

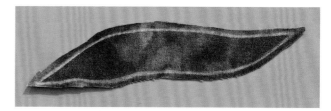

2. Appliqué the center edge of the C-1 piece to a piece of fabric large enough for the vein.

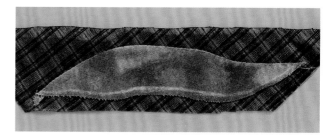

3. Cut the vein fabric ¼" from your stitched line and lift up shape C-1 to finish cutting the remaining seam allowance underneath even with the seam allowance of C-1.

4. Turn under and finger-press a fold along the vein fabric, so that only about ¹⁄₁₆" is visible. Stitch the folded vein to a piece of fabric that is large enough to hold shape C-2. Press template C-2 right next to your first stitched line, *over* the vein, and mark around it. Remove the freezer paper and cut a ³⁄₁₆ " seam allowance around the C-2 shape, lifting up piece C-1 when you need to cut the seam allowance underneath even with the seam allowance of the vein.

5. Continue as established to stitch the remaining C-3/C-4 leaf.

CENTER PETALS AND OVAL

1. Using a fine-point permanent black marking pen, trace the six center petals from pages 72 and 73 onto the dull side of a piece of freezer paper. Cut out each template and press them onto the right side of your chosen fabrics. Mark around each petal with a removable fabric-marking pencil and cut out each of them with a ³⁄₁₆" seam allowance. Leave the freezer paper on each petal until you are ready to arrange them on your stitched flower petals. Remove the freezer-paper templates just before you stitch each center petal in place.

2. In the same manner as for the center petals, prepare the center oval shape on page 72.

PUTTING IT ALL TOGETHER

Refer to the photo on page 68 to arrange and stitch your completed units and pieces to the background fabric in the following order: stem-with-leaf units, leaves, large flower petals, center petals, and the center oval. Add seed beads or other small beads to the center oval shape, as desired, referring to the tip on page 39.

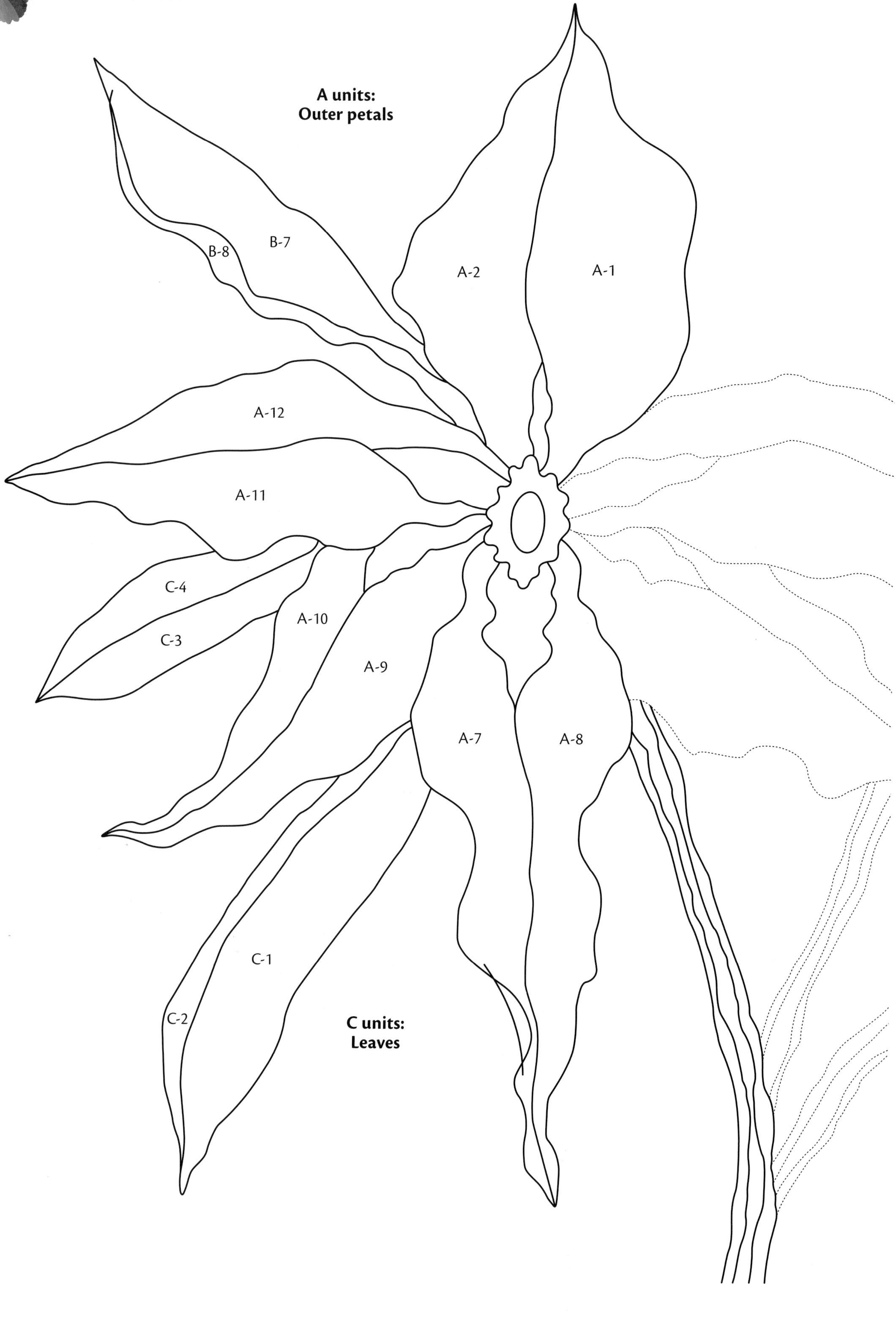

**A units:
Outer petals**

B-8

B-7

A-2

A-1

A-12

A-11

C-4

A-10

C-3

A-9

A-7

A-8

C-1

C-2

**C units:
Leaves**

NOTE
- To make templates, trace the units shown in solid black lines.
- To position units on background fabric, refer to their placements shown on these two pages.

A-4

A-3

A-6

A-5

B-4

B-6

B-5

**B units:
Stems with leaves**

B-1

B-3

B-2

Iris

Stitched by Pat Svitek

Irises come in a wide array of beautiful colors. You can stitch this flower in graduated tints and tones of your favorite color family and add some deep, dark shades for the lower petals and shadows.

TECHNIQUES

Unit appliqué (page 10)

Color blending (page 15)

Free-form stems (page 19)

Inserting a thin band of color (page 20)

Steep outer points (page 21)

FABRICS AND SUPPLIES

▸ Wide assortment of 6" squares of light and dark fabrics for upper and lower flower petals

▸ 9" square of dark fabric for shadowed areas of upper flower petals

▸ Assorted fat quarters of fabrics for stem, leaves, and leaf veins

▸ Assorted 3" squares of dark, medium, and light fabrics for calyx

A UNIT: FLOWER

1. Using a fine-point permanent black marking pen, trace the entire flower unit from pages 80 and 81 onto the dull side of a piece of freezer paper, including the shaded areas. Mark the letter and number on each petal piece and fill in the shaded areas. Cut out the unit along the outer edges.

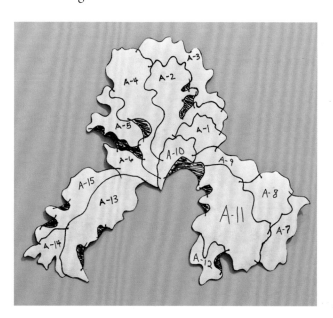

2. Cut the template into three sections. The first section should include pieces A-1 through A-6; the second section should include pieces A-7 through A-12; and the third section should include pieces A-13 through A-15.

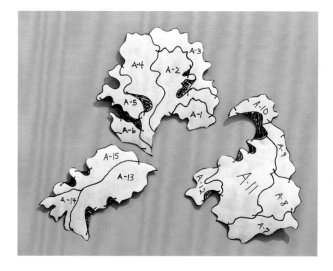

3. Cut out template A-1 and press it onto the right side of your chosen fabric. Using a fabric-marking pencil, mark around the template, including the two hatch marks that indicate where piece A-1 touches piece A-2. Remove the freezer-paper template and cut out piece A-1 with a 3/16" seam allowance. Appliqué the top edge of piece A-1 between the hatch marks to a piece of fabric that is large enough to hold shape A-2.

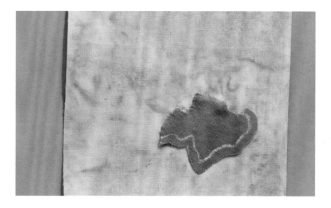

4. Cut template A-2 from the freezer-paper pattern. Cut out the two small shaded areas on piece A-2 and lay them aside temporarily. Press the A-2 template next to your stitched line on piece A-1 and mark around it, including the hatch marks. Remove the freezer-paper template and

cut a ³⁄₁₆" seam allowance around piece A-2, lifting up piece A-1 when you need to cut the seam allowance of A-2 even with the seam allowance of A-1. Clip the seam allowance at the hatch marks.

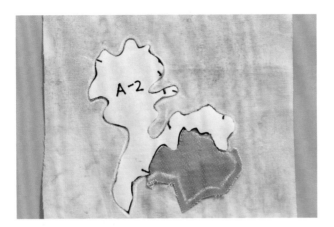

5. Pin a square of dark fabric underneath the A-1/A-2 unit. Appliqué the A-2 piece to the dark fabric between the two sets of hatch marks for the two shaded areas. Using a fabric-marking pencil, mark a slightly curved line on the fabric for the turning lines of these shaded areas.

6. Appliqué the right edge of piece A-2, including the shaded areas, to a piece of fabric large enough to hold piece A-3. Cut piece A-3 from the freezer-paper template and press it next to your stitched line on piece A-2. Mark around the A-3 template. Remove the freezer-paper

template and cut a ³⁄₁₆" seam allowance around piece A-3, lifting up piece A-2 when you need to cut the seam allowance underneath it.

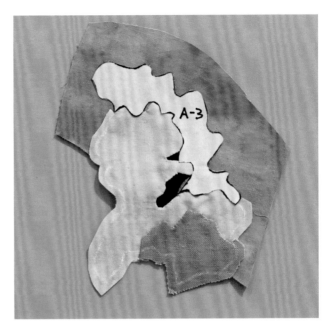

7. Continue as established, adding pieces A-4, A-5, and A-6 to complete this petal section.

8. In the same manner, stitch petal section A-7 through A-12 and petal section A-13 through A-15, including the shaded areas in each section.

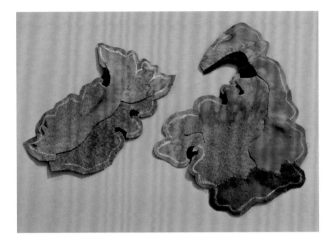

9. Appliqué the top edge of pieces A-9/A-10 between the hatch marks to the top petal section. Appliqué the bottom edge of piece A-6 to the left-hand flower section between the outermost hatch marks.

B UNIT: STEM

1. Cut a strip of fabric on the bias that measures about ⅜" x 6", allowing the edges to be slightly uneven. Appliqué one of the long edges of this strip to a larger piece of fabric for the center portion of the stem. You can stitch this seam along the bias of the fabric, or to any area of the fabric that has the color you want for the second part of the stem.

2. Cut the larger piece of fabric to about ¼" from the stitched seam, allowing the edge to be slightly uneven. Lift up the first piece to cut the seam allowance underneath.

3. Appliqué the edge of the second strip to a larger piece of fabric for the third portion of the stem and repeat step 2 to cut the seam allowance around it as before.

C UNIT: CALYX

1. Using a fine-point permanent black marking pen, trace the entire calyx unit from page 80 onto the dull side of a piece of freezer paper, including the letters and numbers. Cut piece C-1 from the freezer-paper template and press it onto the right side of your chosen fabric.

Using a fabric-marking pencil, mark around the C-1 template, including the hatch mark. Remove the freezer-paper template and cut a ³⁄₁₆" seam allowance around shape C-1. Clip the seam allowance at the hatch mark.

2. Appliqué the top edge of piece C-1 to a piece of fabric large enough to hold piece C-2, ending at the hatch mark. Cut out the template for piece C-2 from the freezer-paper template and press it next to your stitched line on piece C-1. Using a fabric-marking pencil, mark around template C-2, including the hatch mark. Remove the freezer paper and cut out piece C-2 with a ³⁄₁₆" seam allowance. Lift C-1 to cut the seam allowance of C-2 even with the seam allowance of C-1. Clip the seam allowance at the hatch mark.

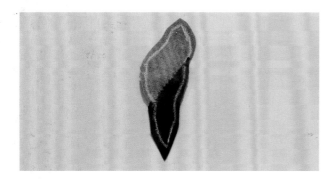

3. Continue as established to add pieces C-3 and C-4 to the unit. This completes the right half of the calyx.

4. Stitch the left half of the calyx from pieces C-5 through C-8.

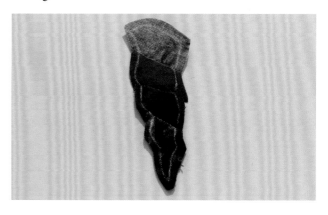

5. Appliqué the right half of the calyx to the left half along the center to complete the calyx unit.

D Units: Leaves

1. Using a fine-point permanent black marking pen, trace the D-1/D-2 leaf from page 80 onto the dull side of a piece of freezer paper, including the letters and numbers. Cut out the template along the outer edges, and then cut apart the leaf along the center line. Press template D-1 onto your chosen fabric. Using a fabric-marking pencil, mark around the template. Remove the freezer-paper template and cut out piece D-1 with a ³⁄₁₆" seam allowance. Appliqué the center edge of piece D-1 to a piece of fabric large enough for the vein.

2. Cut the vein fabric ¼" from your stitched line, allowing it to be slightly uneven. Lift up piece D-1 when you need to cut the seam allowance underneath it.

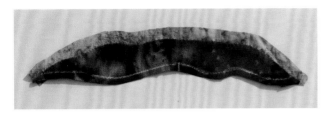

3. Press the D-2 template *over* the vein and right next to your first stitched line on piece D-1 and mark around it with the fabric-marking pencil. Remove the freezer paper and cut a ³⁄₁₆" seam allowance around shape D-2, lifting piece D-1 to cut the seam allowance underneath it even with the seam allowance of the vein.

4. Continue as established to make the remaining four leaf units.

PUTTING IT ALL TOGETHER

Refer to the photo on page 74 to arrange and stitch your completed units and pieces to the background fabric in the following order, referring to "Steep Outer Points" on page 21 to stitch the leaves: stem unit, leaf units, flower unit, and calyx unit.

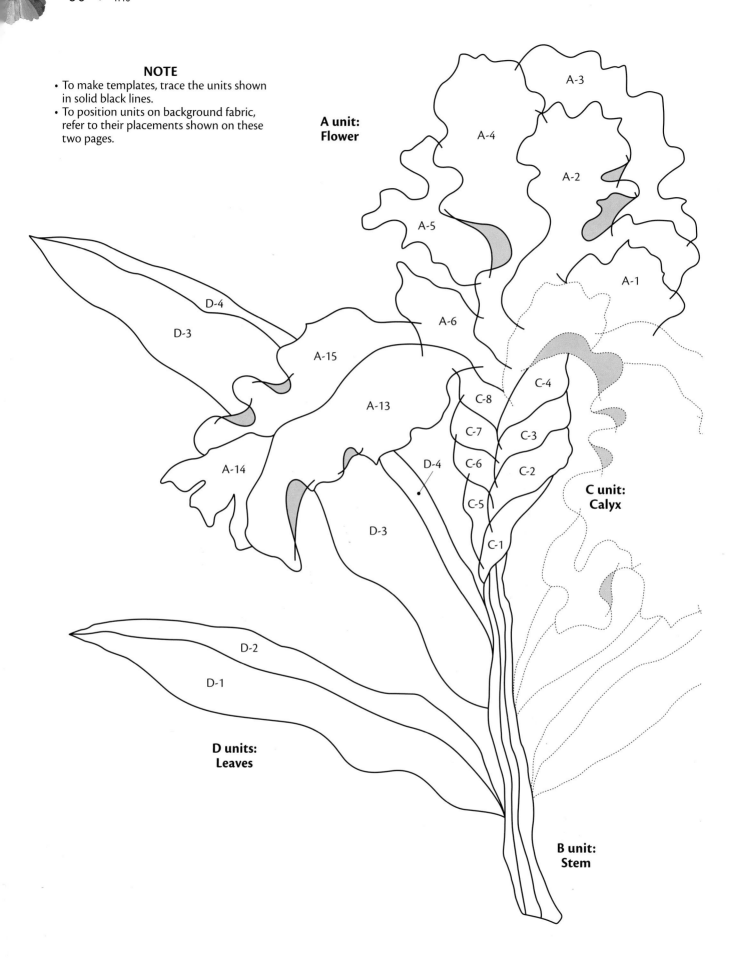

NOTE
- To make templates, trace the units shown in solid black lines.
- To position units on background fabric, refer to their placements shown on these two pages.

A unit: Flower

A-3

A-4

A-2

A-5

A-1

A-6

A-15

C-8

C-4

A-13

C-7

C-3

D-4

C-6

C-2

A-14

C-5

D-3

C-1

C unit: Calyx

D-2

D-1

D units: Leaves

B unit: Stem

Stitched by Heather Semet

Aptly named, these little flowers resemble tiny dancing slippers. Use your favorite colors for the petals, keeping the color values very similar from piece to piece to blend them together effectively, and use a darker color for the inside area of each flower for the look of three-dimensionality.

TECHNIQUES

Unit appliqué (page 10)

Color blending (page 15)

Steep outer points (page 20)

FABRICS AND SUPPLIES

▸ Wide assortment of 3" squares or scraps of fabrics for petals and stamens

▸ 3 squares, 3", or scraps of fabrics for insides of flowers

▸ 2 or more fat quarters of fabric for small leaves surrounding flowers (These can be stitched in shades of green, if desired.)

▸ Assorted fat quarters of fabric for large leaves

▸ Decorative yarn for embellishments (optional)

▸ 100-denier silk thread to match or blend with decorative yarn (if used)

A UNITS: FLOWERS

1. Using a fine-point permanent black marking pen, trace the A-1 through A-8 flower unit from page 85 onto the dull side of a piece of freezer paper and cut it out along the outer edges. Cut piece A-1 from the template and press it onto the right side of your chosen fabric. Using a fabric-marking pencil, mark around piece A-1, including all four hatch marks. Remove the freezer-paper template and cut out piece A-1 with a 3/16" seam allowance around it. Clip the seam allowance at each hatch mark.

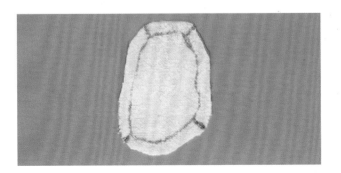

2. Appliqué the left edge of piece A-1, between the hatch marks, to a piece of fabric large enough to hold piece A-2.

3. Cut piece A-2 from the freezer-paper template and press it next to your stitched line on piece A-1. Using a fabric-marking pencil, mark around piece A-2. Remove the freezer-paper template and cut a 3/16" seam allowance around piece A-2, lifting up the A-1 shape when you need to cut the seam allowance underneath it even with the seam allowance of A-1.

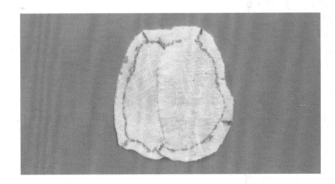

4. Continue as established, adding pieces A-4, A-5, and A-6 to the unit. Pin a 3" square of dark fabric underneath the tops of the petals and appliqué the top edges of the petals to this fabric for the inside of the flower. Finally, add the A-8 stamen piece to complete the flower unit.

5. Stitch the remaining flower units.

B UNITS: LEAVES

There are two types of leaves in this project: the larger leaves with stems and the smaller leaves surrounding the flowers. They are all made in the same manner, but you may use different colors for each type, if you like.

1. Using a fine-point permanent black marking pen, trace the B-1/B-2 leaf from page 85 onto the dull side of a piece of freezer paper, including the letters and numbers. Cut out the template along the outer edges, and then cut apart the leaf along the center line. Press template B-1 onto the right side of your chosen fabric and mark around it using a fabric-marking pencil. Remove the freezer paper and cut out piece B-1 with a 3/16" seam allowance. Appliqué piece B-1 to a piece of fabric large enough to hold piece B-2.

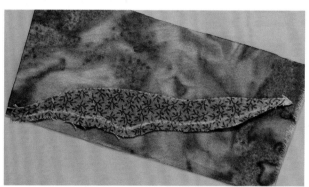

2. Press the B-2 template next to your stitched line and mark around it with a fabric-marking pencil. Remove the freezer-paper template and cut a 3/16" seam allowance around piece B-2, lifting up piece B-1 when you need to cut the seam allowance underneath it.

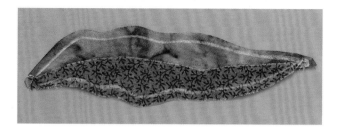

3. Complete the remaining 17 leaf units, using the same process you used to complete the first leaf unit.

PUTTING IT ALL TOGETHER

Refer to the photo on page 82 to arrange and stitch your completed units and pieces to the background fabric in the following order, referring to "Steep Outer Points" on page 21 to stitch the leaves: large leaf units with stems, small leaf units around flowers, followed by the flower units (and any desired yarn embellishment).

NOTE
- To make templates, trace the units shown in solid black lines.
- To position units on background fabric, refer to their placements shown on pages 85 and 86.

**B units:
Leaves**

B-19   B-20

B-22

B-18   B-17

B-25

B-21

A-8

A-4   A-7   A-6

B-24

A-3   A-5

B-23

A-2   A-1

B-14

B-13

B-16

B-12

B-15

B-11

A-25

B-21

A-24   A-23

A-19

A-22

A-18

A-21

B-8

A-17   A-20   B-7

B-6

B-5

**A units:
Flowers**

B-10   B-14

B-3

B-6

B-9

B-4

B-2

B-5

B-1

B-21

B-26

B-27

B-29

B-31

B-30

B-28

B-33

B-32

A-16

A-14

A-15

A-11

A-13

A-12

A-10

A-9

B-35

B-34

B-32

B-26

B-28

Stitched by Pat Svitek

Colombian orchids have exotic, fluid petal shapes. Stitch this pair of blooms in your favorite colors, keeping the shaded parts of the flowers in darker colors than the rest of the flowers.

TECHNIQUES

Unit appliqué (page 10)

Color blending (page 15)

Free-form stems (page 19)

Steep outer points (page 21)

FABRICS AND SUPPLIES

▸ Wide assortment of 6" squares or scraps of fabrics for petals

▸ 2 squares, 4", of fabric for stamens

▸ 2 squares, 2", of fabric for stamen tops

▸ Assorted 6" squares of fabrics for leaves

▸ 3 fat quarters of fabrics for stems

▸ 3" x 5" piece of fabric for base

A UNITS: FLOWERS

The orchids for this block are made in five parts: first comes the top petal unit, then the middle petal unit, followed by the bottom petal unit, the back petal unit, and finally, the stamen. Wait to stitch all the flower units together until you are ready to stitch them onto the background fabric.

1. Using a fine-point permanent black marking pen, trace the top petal unit, A-1 through A-5, from page 92 onto the dull side of a piece of freezer paper. Cut out the entire unit along the outer edges. Cut petal A-1 from the freezer-paper template and press it onto the right side of your chosen fabric. With a fabric-marking pencil, mark around piece A-1, including the two hatch marks at the top. Remove the freezer-paper template and cut a ³⁄₁₆" seam allowance around piece A-1. Clip the seam allowance at the hatch marks.

2. Beginning at the hatch mark on the left side and working toward the bottom of the shape, appliqué piece A-1 to a piece of fabric large enough to hold piece A-2.

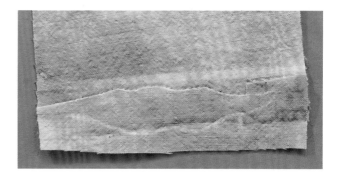

3. Cut piece A-2 from the freezer-paper template, and press it onto the right side of the fabric, next to your stitched line on piece A-1; make sure the hatch marks are aligned. Mark around the A-2 template, including the hatch mark. Cut a ³⁄₁₆" seam allowance around piece A-2, lifting up piece A-1 to cut the seam allowance underneath even with the seam allowance of A-1.

4. Continue as established, adding pieces A-3 through A-5 to the top petal unit.

5. Using a fine-point permanent black marking pen, trace the middle petal unit, A-6 and A-7, from page 92 onto the dull side of a piece of freezer paper, connecting the shapes behind the stamen. Cut out the entire unit along the outer edges, and then cut the pieces apart along the center line.

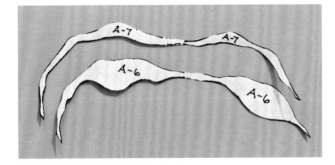

6. Following the cutting and stitching process in steps 1–3, stitch the A-6/A-7 middle petal unit.

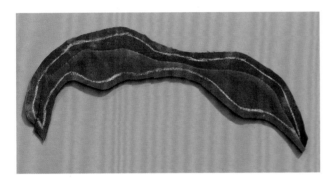

7. Starting with piece A-8 and ending with piece A-12, stitch the bottom petal unit.

8. Using a fine-point permanent black marking pen, trace the back petal unit, A-13 and A-14, from page 92 onto the dull side of a piece of freezer paper, connecting the pieces behind the top petal unit. Cut out the entire unit around the outer edges, and then cut the A-14 pieces from the A-13 piece. Referring to steps 1–3, stitch the back petal unit.

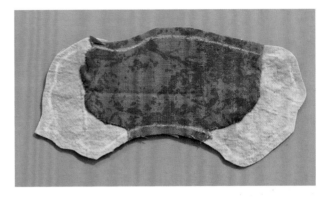

9. Make the freezer-paper templates and stitch the A-15/A-16 stamen unit in the same manner as the petal units.

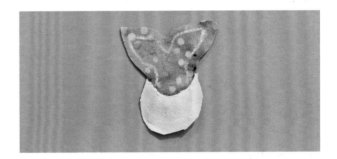

10. Make the units for the second orchid using the same process for the first flower and the pattern on page 92 for pieces A-17 through A-35.

B UNITS: STEMS

1. Cut a strip of fabric on the bias that measures about
⅜" x 18", allowing the long edges to be slightly uneven.
Appliqué one of the long edges of this strip along the
bias of a piece of fabric for the center portion of the stem,
allowing it to be slightly uneven and clipping the seam
allowance of the fabric wherever you wish to stitch an
inner curve.

2. Cut the fabric for the second piece of the stem about
¼" from your stitched seam, allowing the edge to be
slightly uneven. Lift up the first piece to cut the seam
allowance underneath to ³⁄₁₆".

    Appliqué the edge of the second strip to a piece of
fabric for the third portion of the stem and cut the fabric
to ¼" from your stitched line. Cut the 18" stem into three
pieces in the following lengths: 2½", 4", and 11".

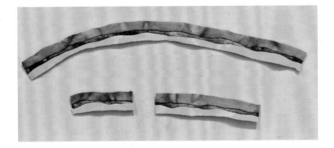

C UNITS: LEAVES

1. Using a fine-point permanent black marking pen,
trace the C-1/C-2 leaf from page 92 onto the dull side
of a piece of freezer paper, including the letters and
numbers. Cut out the entire template along the outer
edges, and then cut it apart along the center line. Press
template C-1 onto the right side of your chosen fabric
and mark around it using a fabric-marking pencil.
Remove the freezer-paper shape and cut out piece C-1
with a ³⁄₁₆" seam allowance around it. Appliqué piece
C-1 to a piece of fabric large enough to hold piece C-2.

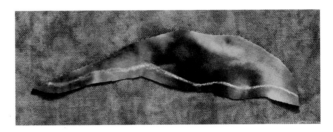

2. Press the C-2 template next to your stitched line and
mark around it with a fabric-marking pencil. Remove
the freezer paper and cut a ³⁄₁₆" seam allowance around
piece C-2, lifting up piece C-1 when you need to cut
the seam allowance underneath even with the seam
allowance of C-1.

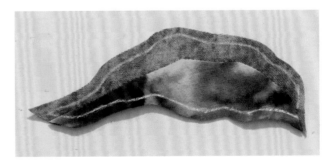

3. Continuing as established, make the remaining six
leaf units.

FLOWER BASE

Using a fine-point permanent black marking pen, trace the flower base from page 92 onto the dull side of a piece of freezer paper. Cut out the template for the flower base along the outer edge and press it onto the right side of your chosen fabric. Mark around the template using a fabric-marking pencil. Remove the freezer paper and cut out the flower base with a 3⁄16" seam allowance around it.

PUTTING IT ALL TOGETHER

Refer to the photo on page 87 to arrange and stitch your completed units and pieces to the background fabric in the following order, referring to "Steep Outer Points" on page 21 to stitch the leaves: stem units, leaf units, flower back units, flower top units, flower middle units, flower bottom units, flower middle units, stamen units, and flower base.

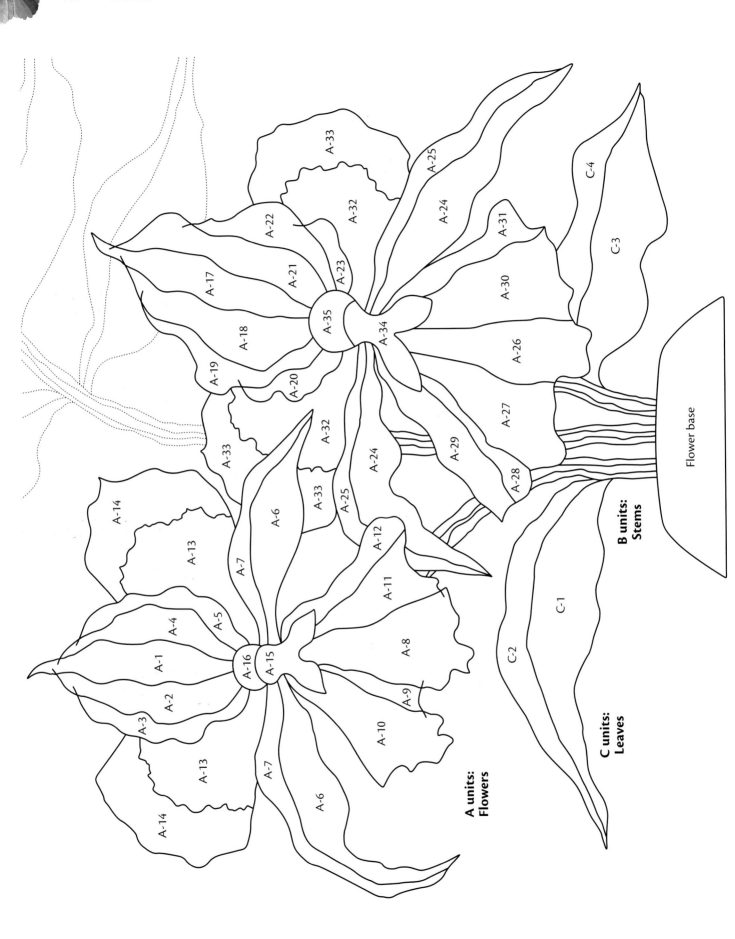

A-33
A-25
C-4
A-22
A-32
A-24
C-3
A-17
A-21
A-23
A-31
A-18
A-35
A-34
A-30
A-19
A-20
A-26
A-33
A-32
A-27
A-14
A-33
A-24
A-29
A-13
A-6
A-33
A-25
A-28
A-4
A-5
A-7
A-12
A-1
A-16
A-11
A-2
A-15
A-8
A-3
C-1
A-9
A-13
A-7
A-10
C-2
A-14
A-6

Flower base

B units:
Stems

A units:
Flowers

C units:
Leaves

NOTE
- To make templates, trace the units shown in solid black lines.
- To position units on background fabric, refer to their placements shown on these two pages.

Pansies

Stitched by Cathy Kucenski

Is there any flower cuter than a pansy? These little blossoms take in sunlight and wave their cheerful petals toward everyone who glances their way.

TECHNIQUES

Unit appliqué (page 10)

Color blending (page 15)

Steep outer points (page 21)

FABRICS AND SUPPLIES

▸ Wide assortment of 6" squares or scraps of fabrics for flower and bud petals

▸ 3 squares, 3", of fabric for large pansy center pieces

▸ Assorted 4" squares or fat quarters of fabrics for leaves

▸ Assorted fat quarter or large scraps of fabric for stems

A UNITS: FLOWERS

1. Using a fine-point permanent black marking pen, trace the large flower unit, pieces A-1 through A-10, from page 99 onto the dull side of a piece of freezer paper. Cut out the entire template along the outer edges. Cut out template A-1/A-2 from the freezer-paper template, and then cut the pieces apart along the line between them. Press template A-1 onto the right side of your chosen fabric and mark around it using a fabric-marking pencil. Remove the freezer-paper template and cut out piece A-1 with a 3/16" seam allowance around it.

2. Appliqué the curved outer petal edge of piece A-1 to a piece of fabric large enough to hold piece A-2. Press template A-2 next to your stitched line on piece A-1.

Using a fabric-marking pencil, mark around piece A-2. Remove the freezer paper and cut a 3/16" seam allowance around piece A-2, lifting up piece A-1 to cut the seam allowance underneath even with the seam allowance of A-1.

3. Continuing as established, stitch the remaining petal units from piece A-3 through piece A-10 into pairs. Stitch the sides of the units together, referring to the pattern on page 99. Add the three center motifs to the center of the stitched petal unit.

4. Using a fine-point permanent black marking pen, trace the petals for the medium pansy, pieces A-11 through A-14, from page 98 onto the dull side of a piece of freezer paper. Do not trace the calyx pieces; these will be added separately. Cut out the entire template along the outer edges, and then cut template A-11 from the template and press it onto the right side of your chosen fabric. Mark around the A-11 template, including the hatch marks; remove the template and cut out piece A-11 with a ³/₁₆" seam allowance. Clip the seam allowance at the hatch marks.

5. Starting at the hatch mark on the left edge and ending at the lower edge of piece A-11, appliqué piece A-11 onto a piece of fabric large enough to hold template A-12. Cut the A-12 template from the flower template and press it onto the fabric, right next to your stitched line on piece A-11. Using a fabric-marking pencil, mark around piece A-12. Remove the freezer-paper template and cut out piece A-12, lifting up piece A-11 to cut the seam allowance underneath it even with the seam allowance of A-11.

6. Add pieces A-13 and A-14 to the medium flower unit.

7. Referring to the cutting and stitching process for the large and medium flower units, stitch the left and right buds.

B Units: Stems

Using a fine-point permanent black marking pen, trace the four stems from pages 98 and 99 onto the dull side of a piece of freezer paper, including the letters and numbers at the bottom of each stem. Cut out the templates along the outer edges. Press these templates onto the right sides of your chosen fabrics. Using a fabric-marking pencil, mark around each stem. Cut out the four stems with a ³⁄₁₆" seam allowance.

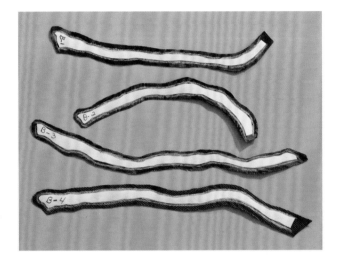

C Units: Leaves

1. Using a fine-point permanent black marking pen, trace the C-1/C-2 leaf from page 98 onto the dull side of a piece of freezer paper, including the letters and numbers. Cut out the template along the outer edges, and then cut apart the templates along the center line. Press template C-1 onto the right side of your chosen fabric and mark around it using a fabric-marking pencil. Remove the freezer-paper template and cut out piece C-1 with a ³⁄₁₆" seam allowance around it. Appliqué piece C-1 to a piece of fabric that is large enough to hold piece C-2.

2. Press the C-2 template next to your stitched line on C-1 and mark around it with a fabric-marking pencil. Remove the freezer paper and cut a ³⁄₁₆" seam allowance around piece C-2, lifting up piece C-1 when you need to cut the seam allowance underneath it even with the seam allowance of C-1.

3. Refer to the cutting and stitching process in steps 1 and 2 to make the remaining nine leaf units.

Calyxes

Using a fine-point permanent black marking pen, trace the calyxes on the smaller flower and buds from pages 98 and 99 onto the dull side of a piece of freezer paper. Cut out each piece and press it onto the right side of your chosen fabric. Mark around the freezer-paper templates. Remove the freezer-paper templates and cut out each piece with a ³⁄₁₆" seam allowance around it. Lay these pieces aside until you are ready to stitch them onto the background fabric.

Putting It All Together

Refer to the photo on page 94 to arrange and stitch your completed units and pieces to the background fabric in the following order, referring to "Steep Outer Points" on page 21 to stitch the leaves: stems and leaf units (take note of overlapping and underlapping pieces as you stitch these pieces onto the background fabric), large pansy unit, smaller pansy unit, bud units, and calyxes.

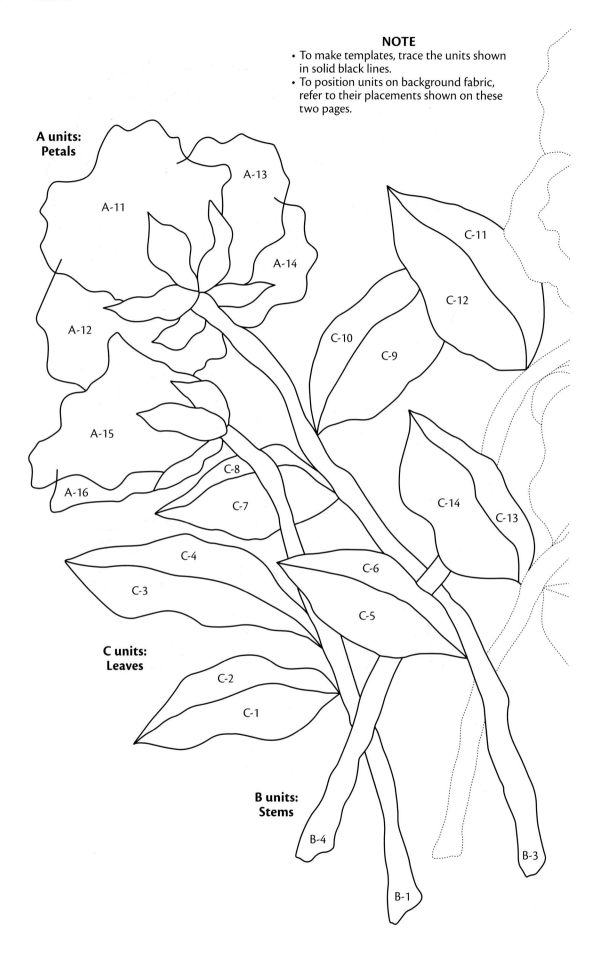

NOTE
- To make templates, trace the units shown in solid black lines.
- To position units on background fabric, refer to their placements shown on these two pages.

A units: Petals

A-13

A-11

A-14

A-12

A-15

A-16

C units: Leaves

C-11

C-12

C-10

C-9

C-8

C-7

C-4

C-3

C-14

C-13

C-6

C-5

C-2

C-1

B units: Stems

B-4

B-3

B-1

Stitched by Pat Svitek

You can stitch these sweet peas in any colors you like; keep the color values between adjacent pieces very similar for a color-blended look.

TECHNIQUES

Unit appliqué (page 10)

Color blending (page 15)

Free-form stems and branches (page 19)

Inserting a thin band of color (page 20)

Steep outer points (page 21)

FABRICS AND SUPPLIES

▶ Wide assortment of 6" squares or large scraps of fabric in two color families for the sweet peas

▶ Three 12" squares or fat quarters of fabrics for the stems and leaves

▶ One 12" square of fabric for the leaf veins

▶ Embroidery floss for tendrils

▶ Embroidery needle

A UNIT: RIGHT FLOWER

1. Using a fine-point permanent black marking pen, trace pieces A-1 through A-7 from page 106 onto the dull side of a piece of freezer paper, including the hatch marks. Cut out the entire template along the outer edges, and then cut the two halves of the template apart, separating pieces A-1 through A-4 from pieces A-5 through A-7.

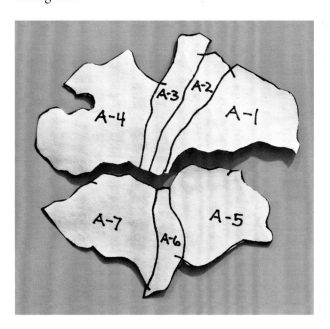

2. Cut piece A-1 from the freezer-paper template and press it onto the right side of your chosen fabric. Using a fabric-marking pencil, mark around template A-1, including the hatch mark. Remove the freezer-paper template and cut a ³⁄₁₆" seam allowance around piece A-1. Clip the seam allowance at the hatch mark.

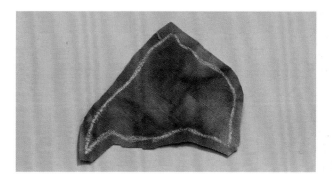

3. Starting at the hatch mark, appliqué the left edge of piece A-1 to a piece of fabric large enough to hold piece A2.

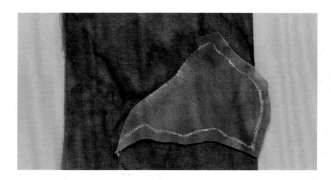

4. Cut template A-2 from the freezer-paper template and press it next to your seam line on piece A-1, making sure that the top right corner of piece A-2 aligns with the beginning of your seam line.

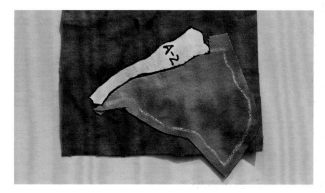

5. Mark around template A-2. Remove the freezer-paper template and cut out piece A-2 with a ³⁄₁₆" seam allowance around it, lifting up piece A-1 to cut the seam allowance underneath it even with the seam allowance of piece A-1.

6. Continue as established, adding pieces A-3 and A-4 to the unit.

7. Appliqué pieces A-5 through A-7 of the lower unit together using the same stitching method as for the upper flower unit.

8. Appliqué the lower unit over the bottom edge of the upper unit, starting and ending at the hatch marks on pieces A-5 and A-7.

B Unit: Bud

Using the same marking, cutting, and stitching methods as for "A Unit: Right Flower," stitch together pieces B-1 through B-4 for the bud.

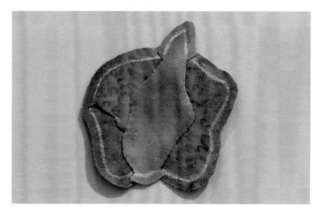

C UNIT: LEFT FLOWER

Referring to the marking, cutting, and stitching methods for "A Unit: Right Flower," stitch together the upper part of the left sweet pea, pieces C-1 through C-3, and then add the two small shadowed areas, pieces C-4 and C-5. For the lower flower unit, stitch together pieces C-6 and C-7. For the small side unit at the bottom left of the flower, stitch together pieces C-8 through C-11. Stitch the lower unit of C-6/C-7 over the bottom edge of the top unit of pieces C-1 through C-5. Stitch the C-6 piece to the side unit of pieces C-8 through C-11.

D UNITS: STEMS

1. Cut a strip of fabric on the bias that measures about ⅜" x 9", allowing the edges to be slightly uneven. Appliqué one long edge of this strip to a piece of fabric large enough to hold the second portion of the stem. You can stitch this seam either along the bias of the fabric, or in any area of the fabric that has the color you want for the second part of the stem.

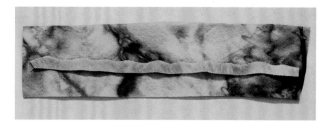

2. Cut the larger piece of fabric to about ¼" from the seam line, allowing this cut to be slightly uneven. Lift up the first piece to cut a ³⁄₁₆" seam allowance underneath it.

3. Repeat to make a total of four two-part stems.

E UNITS: LEAVES

1. Using a fine-point permanent black marking pen, trace the E-1/E-2 leaf from page 106 onto the dull side of a piece of freezer paper, including the letters and numbers. Cut out the template along the outer edges, and then cut it apart along the center line. Press template E-1 onto the right side of your chosen fabric and mark around it using a fabric-marking pencil. Remove the freezer paper and cut out piece E-1 with a ³⁄₁₆" seam allowance around it. Appliqué piece E-1 to a piece of fabric large enough to hold a center vein.

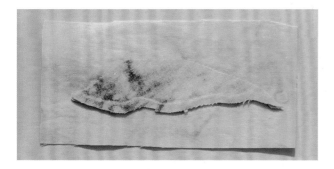

2. Cut the vein fabric to ¼" from your stitched line. Lift up the E-1 piece to cut the seam allowance underneath even with the seam allowance of piece E-1.

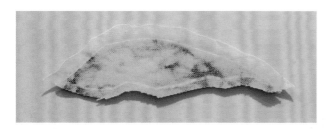

3. Turn under the vein fabric to ¹⁄₁₆" and finger-press the fold. Sew the folded edge of the vein fabric to a piece of fabric large enough to hold piece E-2.

4. Press the E-2 template next to your first stitched line *over* the vein, on piece E-1. Mark around the E-2 template with a fabric-marking pencil. Remove the freezer paper and cut a ³⁄₁₆" seam allowance around piece E-2, lifting up piece E-1 when you need to cut the seam allowance underneath it even with the seam allowance of the vein.

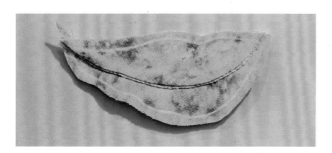

5. Make the remaining three leaves as established.

PUTTING IT ALL TOGETHER

Refer to the photo on page 100 and arrange and stitch your completed units and pieces to the background fabric in the following order, referring to "Steep Outer Points" on page 21 to stitch the leaves: stem units, leaf units, and sweet pea and bud units. Trace the tendril lines onto the block background. Follow the lines to stem stitch the tendrils using two or three strands of embroidery floss.

Stem stitch

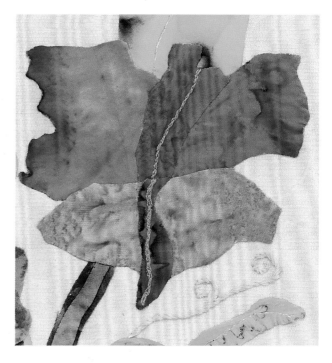

NOTE
- To make templates, trace the units shown in solid black lines.
- To position units on background fabric, refer to their placements shown on pages 105 and 106.

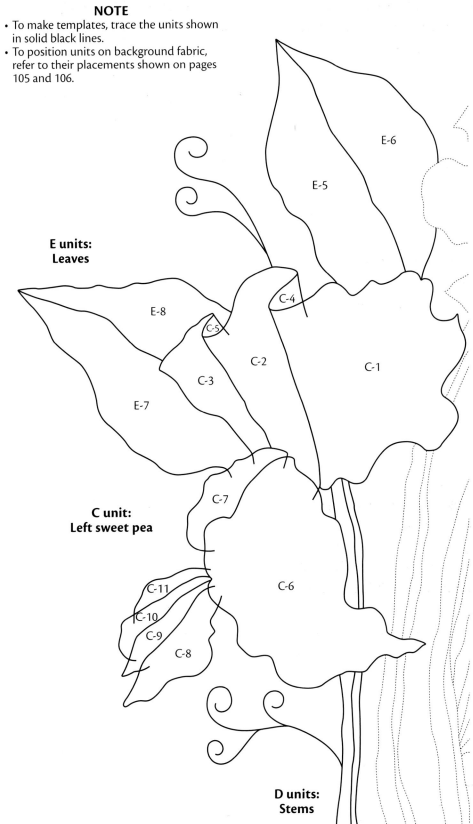

**E units:
Leaves**

**C unit:
Left sweet pea**

**D units:
Stems**

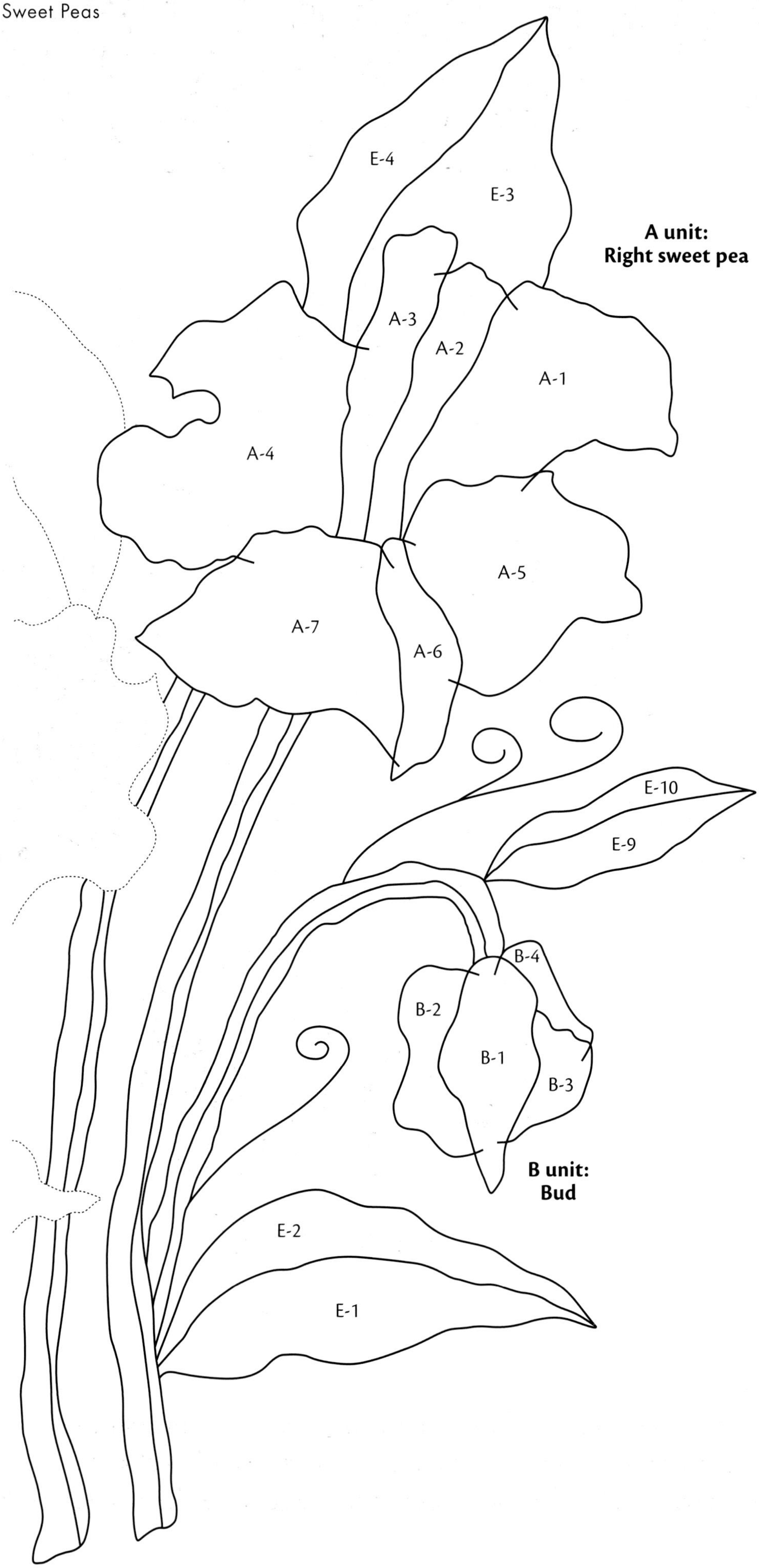

E-4

E-3

A unit:
Right sweet pea

A-3

A-2

A-1

A-4

A-5

A-7

A-6

E-10

E-9

B-4

B-2

B-1

B-3

B unit:
Bud

E-2

E-1

Stitched by Pat Svitek

Tulips are some of the most classically beautiful flowers in nature, with smooth, shiny petals that gleam in the sun. Whatever colors you choose for these three flowers, keep the color values similar in adjacent pieces to create a color-blended effect and choose a contrast color for the inside of the flowers.

TECHNIQUES

Unit appliqué (page 10)

Color blending (page 15)

Scrappliqué (page 17)

Inserting a thin band of color (page 20)

Steep outer points (page 21)

FABRICS AND SUPPLIES

▸ Wide assortment of 6" squares or scraps of fabrics for flowers

▸ 2 or 3 fat quarters of fabrics for stems and leaves

▸ 1 fat quarter of fabric for leaf veins

▸ Two colors of yarn for embellishing stems

A UNITS: FLOWERS

1. Using a fine-point permanent black marking pen, trace the tulip on the left, pieces A-1 through A-8, from page 111 onto the dull side of a piece of freezer paper. Cut out the entire template along the outer edges. Cut out piece A-1 from the template and press it onto the right side of your chosen fabric. Using a fabric-marking pencil, mark around the template, including all four hatch marks. Remove the freezer-paper template and cut out piece A-1 with a ³/₁₆" seam allowance. Clip the seam allowance at the hatch marks.

2. Starting at the top hatch mark on the left and ending at the lower hatch mark on the left edge, appliqué piece A-1 to a piece of fabric large enough to hold piece A-2.

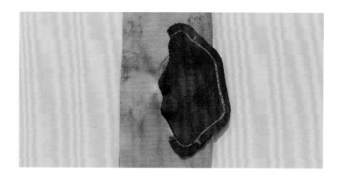

3. Cut template A-2 from the freezer-paper template and press it next to your seam line on piece A-1, between the hatch marks. Using a fabric-marking pencil, mark around piece A-2, including the two hatch marks. Remove the freezer paper and cut a ³/₁₆" seam allowance around piece A-2, lifting up piece A-1 to cut the seam allowance underneath it even with the seam allowance of A-1.

4. Continue as established to add pieces A-3 through A-8 to complete this tulip unit.

5. Using the same marking, cutting, and stitching method, stitch the middle and right tulip units.

B Units: Leaves

1. Trace the B-1/B-2 leaf from page 112 onto the dull side of a piece of freezer paper, including the letters and numbers. Cut out the template along the outer edges, and then cut it apart along the center line. Press template B-1 onto your chosen fabric and mark around it using a fabric-marking pencil. Remove the freezer-paper template and cut out piece B-1 with a ³⁄₁₆" seam allowance around it. Appliqué the center edge of piece B-1 to a piece of fabric large enough to hold a center vein.

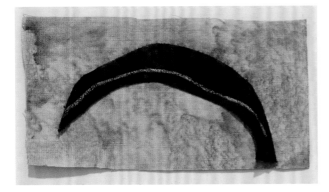

2. Cut the vein fabric to ¼" from your stitched line. Lift up the B-1 piece to cut a ³⁄₁₆" seam allowance underneath it even with the seam allowance of piece B-1.

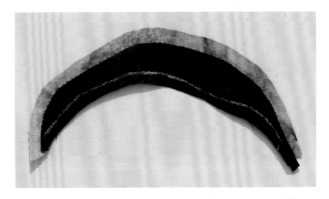

3. Press the B-2 template next to your *first* stitched line, *over* the vein on piece B-1. Mark around the B-2 template with a fabric-marking pencil. Remove the freezer-paper template and cut a ³⁄₁₆" seam allowance around piece B-2, lifting up piece B-1 when you need to cut the seam allowance underneath it even with the seam allowance of the vein.

4. Continue as established to stitch the remaining four leaf units.

Stems

You have the choice of two types of stems: traditional appliquéd stems or twisted stems. The traditional appliqué method will provide a flat stem and the twisted stem will be three-dimensional.

For a traditional appliquéd stem, use a fine-point permanent black marking pen to trace the three stems from page 111 onto the dull side of a piece of freezer paper, including the letters and numbers on each stem. Cut out the templates along the outer edges. Press these templates onto the right sides of your chosen fabrics. Using a fabric-marking pencil, mark around each stem. Cut out the four stems with a ³⁄₁₆" seam allowance. Set the stems aside until you are ready to apply them.

If you wish to make twisted stems, make the stems right before you are ready to apply them. For the long center stem, cut a strip from your chosen fabric that measures about ³⁄₈" x 6". Cut a length of yarn the same length as the fabric strip. Twist the yarn and fabric strip together from one end to the other. Stitch the stem in place on the background fabric. Repeat this process to make two additional stems that are approximately 3" long. When you stitch these stems to the background fabric, one end of each stem will lie underneath the vase and the other end under a tulip.

Scrapliqué Vase

Trace the vase pattern on page 112 onto the dull side of a piece of freezer paper and cut it out. Referring to "Scrapliqué" on page 17 and to the block photo on page 107, stitch together enough scrap fabrics to create a mosaic-like, free-form piece that is large enough for you to press the vase template onto it. Mark around the vase template, remove the freezer paper, and cut out the vase with a ¼" seam allowance around it.

Putting It All Together

Refer to the photo on page 107 to arrange and stitch your completed units and pieces to the background fabric in the following order, referring to "Steep Outer Points" on page 21 to stitch the leaves: appliquéd and/or twisted stems and leaf units (take note of overlapping and underlapping pieces as you stitch these pieces onto the background fabric), tulip units, and scrapliqué vase.

NOTE
- To make templates, trace the units shown in solid black lines.
- To position units on background fabric, refer to their placements shown on pages 111 and 112.

B units:
Leaves

A units:
Tulips

C units:
Stems

B-6

B-5

B-7

B-8

B-9

B-10

B-8

B-7

B-5

C-1

C-2

C-3

A-13

A-12

A-15

A-14

A-16

A-11

A-10

A-9

A-22

A-25

A-23

A-24

A-26

A-19

A-20

A-21

A-18

A-17

A-27

A-5

A-4

A-6

A-1

A-2

A-3

A-7

A-8

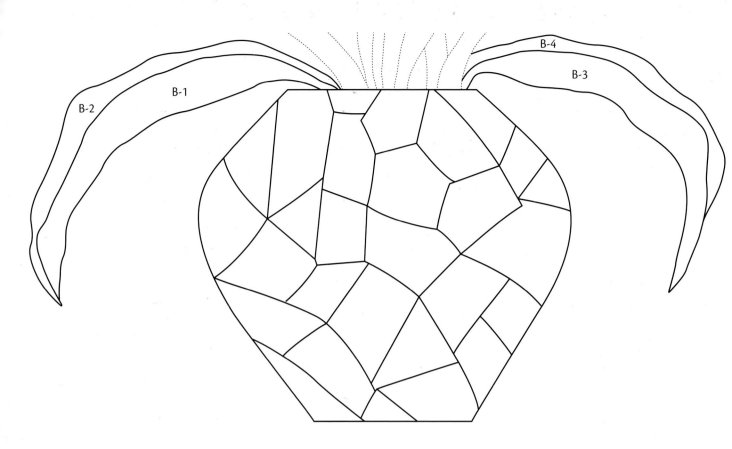

Resources

Gail Kessler
Ladyfingers Sewing Studio
6375 Oley Turnpike Road
Oley, PA 19547
Website: www.ladyfingerssewing.com
Phone: 610-689-0068
Fax: 610-689-0067
General sewing supplies, quilt fabrics, block-of-the-month kits, 3½" serrated embroidery scissors, CAT paper, 100-denier YLI silk thread (all colors), John James needles

Jeana Kimball's Foxglove Cottage
P.O. Box 220
Spring City, UT 84662
Website: www.jeanakimballquilter.com
Phone: 435-462-9618
Size 11 straw needles and extra-sharp appliqué pins

Mickey Lawler's Skydyes
P.O. Box 370116
West Hartford, CT 06137-0116
Email: fabric@skydyes.com
Website: www.skydyes.com
Fax: 860-236-9117
Gorgeous hand-painted fabrics